CHRISTIANESE OR CHRIST?

CHRISTIANESE OR CHRIST?

THE TIMELY CHALLENGE OF
JESUS' PARABLE OF THE SOWER

A Study in Eight Sessions for Pastors, Individuals, or Small Groups.

TIM J. R. TRUMPER

Grand Rapids, Michigan, U.S.A.
Ephesians 3:20 Publishing (Reaching America Ministries)
From His Fullness Ministries
2019

Christianese or Christ? The Timely Challenge of Jesus' Parable of the Sower

© 2019 Tim J. R. Trumper

Published by:

Ephesians 3:20 Publishing
Reaching America Ministries
4180 44th Street, SE
Grand Rapids, MI 49512
United States of America

From His Fullness Ministries
840 Oakhurst Ave., NW
Grand Rapids, MI 49504
United States of America

ISBN: 9781073424740

First printing 2019.

All Scripture quotations, unless otherwise stated, are taken from the English Standard Version, The Large Print Edition (Wheaton, Illinois: Crossway Bibles, 2004).

Front cover image: James J. Tissot, "The Sower" (1886-96), watercolor, Brooklyn Museum, New York.

To Dale and Marcia

". . . beloved fellow workers . . . "

Philemon 1:1

". . . blessed are your eyes, for they see,

and your ears, for they hear."

Matthew 13:16

This is a superb example of the preaching I love, systematic, expository, evangelistic preaching. This Welshman, Dr Timothy Trumper, stands in the succession of preachers exemplified by Dr. Martyn Lloyd-Jones, but his ministry has been expanded by his own keen mind, theological training, international experience, warm spirituality and the utterly contemporary nature of his proclamation of the Lord Jesus Christ. So equipped, he faces ideas and issues that congregations and pulpits have to face. There is much help here for the Christian and also for every pastor as they are introduced to the great Sower who constantly goes forth sowing the seed of the word.

Geoff Thomas

I counsel every learner willingly to lend his ear to the word of God, and to hear with love of the truth what we say, that his mind, receiving the best seed, may bring forth joyful fruits by good deeds. For if, while I teach the things which pertain to salvation, any one refuses to receive them, and strives to resist them with a mind occupied by evil opinions, he shall have the cause of his perishing, not from us, but from himself. For it is his duty to examine with just judgment the things which we say, and to understand that we speak the words of truth, that, knowing how things are, and directing his life in good actions, he may be found a partaker of the kingdom of heaven, subjecting to himself the desires of the flesh, and becoming lord of them, that so at length he himself also may become the pleasant possession of the Ruler of all.

Recognitions of Clement 5:8

The grace of God in the heart of man is a tender plant in a strange, unkindly soil; and therefore cannot well prosper and grow, without much care and pains, and that of a skillful hand, and which hath the art of cherishing it: for this end hath God given the constant ministry of the word to his church, not only for the first work of conversion, but also for confirming and increasing his grace in the hearts of his children.

Robert Leighton, *A Practical Commentary Upon the First Epistle General of Saints Peter*

O Lord, prepare my heart to receive your word, that it may be like the good ground, or I shall be undone for ever. Let my heart be broken up and prepared by your plough. O that I may have a good, an upright and sincere heart.

Benjamin Keach, *Exposition of the Parables*

CONTENTS

ABBREVIATIONS

ESV   English Standard Version of the Bible

KJV   King James Version of the Bible

NKJV New King James Version of the Bible

WCF   Westminster Confession of Faith (1647)

PREFACE

It is estimated a staggering 2,200,000 new book titles or editions are published per year. Unsurprisingly, the United States tops the list with nearly 300,000 titles. My native United Kingdom comes in third (after China) with 149,000.[1] That is great news for authors, publishers, and readers. But in the church, we must ever guard against the usurping of the God-ordained primacy of preaching by the man-made primacy of publication (consider Mark 1:38; Romans 10:14-17; 1 Corinthians 1:21-25).

Jesus, we recall, never wrote a book by his own hand. Our Lord put his ministry efforts into communing with his Father, into preaching, and acts of kindness. He understood, in words my father instilled into me, that, "People have souls, books don't!" Not that books don't communicate to souls, but we can be so busy writing them (or reading them) that we ignore the immediate needs of the people around us. In other words, Jesus never lost sight of his call to minister to those he encountered. This required him to fellowship with men, women, and children; to comfort them by word and deed; and ultimately to die for them. Perhaps, then, we who minister ought to ask each other fewer questions such as, "What are you writing?" or even "Where have you traveled to preach?" preferring instead to ask such questions as, "Which of the lost or the downtrodden have touched your heart and inspired your prayers of late?"; or, "Who in your congregation has recently emboldened your faith or enlarged your hope?"

This is not to demean Christian literature. God has used it greatly and, of course, etched his message indelibly in the veritable library of sixty-six books we call the Bible (better, the Holy Bible).

---

[1] http://en.wikipedia.org/wiki/Books_published_per_country_per_year, accessed on November 30, 2013.

It is the best-selling tome of all time! Uninspired books, too, serve the primacy of preaching. Indeed, every preacher can testify to how books have proved as indispensable to pulpit ministry as tools are to a tradesman. Yet, there is more to life than books, and greatness in the eyes of God—if there is such a concept outside of himself—may be attained in many more ways than by writing books. Our Lord Jesus will assess us on his Day as much by the sharing of food, drink, clothing, and time with the needy as by the number or quality of books written in self-imposed confinement (Matthew 25:31-40).

I make this point, for in the current climate there is a tendency to assume that those who have written the most books and are best known must be the greatest in the kingdom. Jesus teaches us that this is not guaranteed. Consider the notable men and women in Scripture. Many contributed to the canon of Scripture (from the Greek *kanōn*, meaning "rule"), whether by historical accounts, poems, proverbs, books of prophecy, letters, or apocalyptic literature, but few of their lives were preoccupied with writing, let alone with numbering how many books they wrote or sales they achieved. This modern-day equivalent of David counting his armies (2 Samuel 24:1-25; 1 Chronicles 21:1-30) is our preoccupation, but not necessarily the Lord's (Isaiah 55:8).

The Lord does not possess our fascination with the notion of celebrity pastors, nor, indeed, anti-celebrities with their covert hypocrisies and envies. Rather, our Lord Jesus' concern was spiritual: to spread the kingdom of heaven. His honor lay not in currying favor with man, but with pleasing his Father. Everything he did, whether in private or public, was for his Father's glory and expressed his other-person centeredness. Neither celebrities, anti-celebrities, nor would-be celebrities necessarily go to the cross for others. To do so requires a self-forgetful preoccupation with Christ and his kingdom. Wrote Dietrich Bonhoeffer in *The Cost of*

Discipleship, "Only when we have become completely oblivious of self are we ready to bear the cross for his sake."[2]

Given this caution about the preoccupation with publishing, you likely ask, "Why then write a book on the parable of the sower?" After all, the study appears, at first sight, to hold few surprises. The danger of familiarity breeding contempt is real. When, however, we dig into the context of the parable we see just how timely and how searching it is. Indeed, the more I have gone over the parable, the more relevant I have found it to the pressing need of the revival of the church and the awakening of society today.

In it we detect Jesus' poignant countercultural view of ministry and how it stands in contrast to the celebrity and consumerist carnality of our age. The parable's focus on God and his glory, the majestic authority of Christ, and the Word of God as the divine means of accomplishing God's purposes, exposes and refutes today's man-centered and Word-forsaking doing of church. In the words of preacher Benjamin Keach (1640–1704), "One great design of this parable (as I conceive), is to show the excellent nature of the Word of God, in that it is the seed of all grace in the hand of the Spirit; or as it is by the influences of the Spirit, received into an heart prepared by the convictions of the Holy Ghost [Spirit]."[3] The parable, then, is not ultimately about us, our celebrity or wannabe celebrity status, or our consumerism. It is about God and the accomplishment of his saving purposes through his living and written Word.

---

[2] Dietrich Bonhoeffer, *The Cost of Discipleship*, Revised and unabridged edition containing material not previously translated (New York: MacMillan Publishing Co., Inc., 1963), 97.
[3] Benjamin Keach, *Exposition of the Parables*, Series One, reprint ed. (Grand Rapids: Kregel, 1991), 119.

When we take account of this weighty theme running through the context and content of the parable and the powerful lessons it contains pertaining to the disentangling of cultural "Christianity" from biblical Christianity, it is clear that there is more to the parable than meets the eye. Once this dawns on us we can see more clearly why the parable of the sower is the most well-known of those Jesus told. Certainly, it is the longest, and is found in all three synoptic Gospels (Matthew, Mark, and Luke).[4]

For the idea to go to print with the exposition of the parable I am grateful to my friend, Dr. Terry Slachter, executive director of Reaching America Ministries. He was one of a number of regular listeners to the radio broadcast of Seventh Reformed Church, Grand Rapids, Michigan, who often and selflessly encouraged me in the weekly exposition of God's Word. He suggested a book from the sermon series "Hear the Parable of the Sower," not least because it coincided with the emphasis of Reaching America Ministries on the need to spread God's Word throughout the nation.

Convinced of the primacy of preaching, it has taken some years to fulfill my promise. The original sermons were preached as sermons and not as draft chapters. Such multitasking errs methodologically, for sermons are geared toward the ruggedness of the pastoral context. They communicate through the exposition of God's Word his message to his people in the immediacy of the local church family and the personal circumstances of those belonging to it. Chapters, by contrast, need not be expositional and are meant for a more general readership we may never meet.

The preaching of draft chapters also errs spiritually, for instead of prioritizing those to whom we are called, we have decided to look ahead to publication and perhaps, more crassly, to book

---

[4] Matthew, Mark, and Luke are called *synoptic Gospels* since they constitute a synopsis—a general view of the principal parts of the life, ministry, death, and resurrection of Jesus, and possess similarity of order, content, and statement.

sales. Thus, instead of serving undividedly those before us, we use them as unwitting spectators of a literary refinement process. We thereby challenge, if not sacrifice, the primacy, method, force, and local relevance of preaching for the sake of our own productivity. This, too, often results in the supplanting of the quality of preaching for the quantity of book production; of the primacy of preaching in effect for the primacy of publication. I am not saying that multitasking is wrong in itself, but there is a point at which we may, in the process of being efficient stewards of time, begin cutting corners on the principles of preaching and its quality assurance.

Thus, as laborious as it has been to transpose the series from sermons to chapters, providing additional comment along the way, the task serves to safeguard the nature and integrity of preaching. This endeavor is very much in keeping with the parable's emphasis on the preaching of God's Word and has afforded opportunity to state in greater detail the relevance, context, and application of the parable for today.

In the intervening period, the Lord has led me to found From His Fullness—a ministry serving the church through the preaching and teaching of God's Word in and for the global context.[5] In doing so, I was glad to draw from brother Terry's experience of nonprofit ministries and am delighted he now serves as the first chair of our board of directors. He has refreshed my soul and reminded me, consistent with the teaching of the parable, that although sermons seem to vanish into thin air, they in fact fulfill God's purposes, and more than we know. I am, therefore, delighted that our two ministries—Reaching America Ministries and From His Fullness Ministries—can partner in this way to publish this book.

---

[5] Our vision statement reads: "*From His Fullness* envisions God's pleasure in the feeding of the hungriest church leaders and their congregations across the world with the grace and truth of the Living Word, through the written Word."

Naturally, in turning the sermons into a book I have reflected with thankfulness on the faithful congregants of Seventh Reformed Church. These were preached on consecutive Sunday evenings from May 5 through June 9, 2013. In resisting the all-too-common drift away from offering on the Lord's Day an evening sacrifice of praise, such congregants did much to encourage me.[6] Two such attendees were Dale and Marcia Visser—long-standing friends and encouragers to whom I gladly dedicate this book. I do so, with my abiding love, thanks, esteem, and prayers. Eternity will tell how much they have, behind the scenes, served the cause of Christ's kingdom, according to the gifts, desires, and opportunities God has given them. They are an inspiration in how to remain faithful in worship and service amid the current downgrade in commitment to Christ and to the public means of grace, and amid their own personal challenges.[7]

The series of sermons was one the Lord impressed on me at the last moment. Fellow ministers of the Word will know that experience. The feedback, crystallized by the invitation to write this small book, confirms that the prompting was the Lord's. Conscious of the book's limitations, I nevertheless am assured that he has not yet exhausted his purposes for the sermons and will bring glory to himself through them. This is my desire. It is driven by the awareness that the privilege in sowing the seed of God's Word is of his grace alone.

---

[6] For audio recordings of the sermons, visit the website (www.7thref.org) or contact the office of Seventh Reformed Church, 950 Leonard Street, Grand Rapids, MI 49504 ([001] 616-459-4451).

[7] Amid the completion of the final edits, our Lord took Dale home to himself. He died in Grand Rapids on July 15 and was buried here on July 19, 2019. My open letter to Marcia and to her family in personal tribute to Dale is available on our website at http://www.fromhisfullness.com/about/personnel-2/in-memoriam/mr-dale-j-visser/, accessed July 23, 2019. He is sorely missed for both his person and service to Christ's kingdom.

To glean most from the study, take time to appreciate:

- *Contextually*, Jesus' teaching of the theme of the kingdom of heaven and of the working of parables.
- *Vocationally*, Jesus' expectations of the proclamation of the Word of the kingdom.
- *Practically*, Jesus' identification of the reasons why hearers of the Word respond in the way that they do.
- *Spiritually*, Jesus' call to ensure that we are in the kingdom and not simply among the crowd of hangers-on around him.

When considered for its context as well as its content, it is not difficult to see that there is something in the parable for everyone: for the preacher as also for the hearer of the Word, for those inside the kingdom as well as for those yet outside of it.

Sometimes those ministering the Word are addressed. After all, Jesus labels his parable "the parable of the sower" and makes it very clear that it is by the preaching of "the word of the kingdom" that he gathers subjects under his reign (Matthew 13:18-19). On other occasions, I address hearers of the Word (which includes those who preach), for much of Jesus' telling and interpreting of the parable is taken up with the soil on which the seed lands and asks about the state of our hearts when hearing the Word. How, for instance, we hear the Word preached has a significant bearing on what is accomplished through its delivery. The onus in weighing preaching does not fall solely on the preacher.

Then again, the parable leads me to speak to hearers of the Word—sometimes to those belonging to the kingdom and in other instances to those yet to enter it. My purpose is not to dictate to you your standing with God. Not only do I not know who you are or who is reading this, I leave it to the Holy Spirit to use the exposition to comfort or to convict you, as he sees fit. While there is a responsibility that a preacher has to apply the general principles of what a given passage teaches, it is the Spirit, with his divine power and perfect knowledge of the will of God and of the individual hearer, who funnels the study through each of our minds to our hearts and to our wills.

The parable of the sower is, then, a rich network of themes and applications. The exposition reflects this. When we set it against the backdrop of Jesus' ministry (and its narration in the synoptic Gospels, Matthew's especially), we are faced with multiple strands of teaching. Each of these must find their place in the exposition, yet without losing sight of the main two-sided thrust of Jesus' parable: the significance of the preaching and hearing of the Word.

For support in completing the manuscript I am indebted to my wife, Brenda. From the earliest years of our marriage she has worn two hats simultaneously, and three in total thus far. Not only is she my wife, she has served as secretary to the pastor and elders at Seventh Reformed Church and is now manager and member of the board of directors of From His Fullness Ministries. God be praised for her grace, her gifts, and her calling! I honor her for her availability to God, her humility in utilizing her gifts, and her rich ministry of prayer. Indeed, it was her theological and practical insights, expressed with much naturalness, warmth, and clarity in prayer, which were instrumental in no small part in drawing me to her.

I am also encouraged by the feedback of my esteemed brother Doug Brink, an elder of Little Farms Chapel (Orthodox Presbyterian Church), chair of the mission committee, and member of the board of directors of From His Fullness Ministries. It has been a spiritual battle to complete the manuscript for publication, but his feedback has given me the stimulus needed to go the last mile. Furthermore, I am humbled and very grateful to Rev. Geoff Thomas, D.D., erstwhile minister of Alfred Place Baptist Church, Aberystwyth, Wales, for his endorsement of the study. Having ministered fruitfully from the pulpit there for a monumental fifty years (1965–2016), plus internationally throughout those decades, his affirmation of the study is most welcome.

Our dear friend, Marilyn Van Dyke, has most kindly copy-edited the manuscript. We praise God for Marilyn's skill as a first-rate editor, and for her heart in serving her Lord as such. We treasure her person, then her help, but the spirit with which she helps the ministry of From His Fullness bespeaks her person.

It goes without saying that any errors in the exposition are mine and that I own the opinions expressed. They are personal convictions, but I remain open to refinements or corrections of my thinking. And, so, for the parable—Jesus' countercultural view of the ministry of the Word. Thank you for joining me in studying it!

Tim J. R. Trumper
From His Fullness Ministries
www.fromhisfullness.com

THE TEXTS OF THE PARABLE OF THE SOWER

> Often it is only by combining the three independent testimonies that we get a clear and graphic picture.

> Frederic W. Farrar, *The Life of Christ*

Although the parable is familiar, it will help to review it before commencing the study. Pay particular attention to those clauses differing from account to account.

MATTHEW 13:1-23	MARK 4:1-20	LUKE 8:4-15
That same day Jesus went out of the house and sat beside the sea. [2] And great crowds gathered about him, so that he got into a boat and sat down. And the whole crowd stood on the beach. [3] And he told them many things in parables, saying: "A sower went out to sow. [4] And as he sowed, some seeds fell along the path, and the birds came and devoured them. [5] Other seeds fell on rocky ground, where they did not have much soil, and immediately they sprang up, since they had no depth of	Again he began to teach beside the sea. And a very large crowd gathered about him, so that he got into a boat and sat in it on the sea, and the whole crowd was beside the sea on the land. [2] And he was teaching them many things in parables, and in his teaching he said to them: [3] "Listen! A sower went out to sow. [4] And as he sowed, some seed fell along the path, and the birds came and devoured it. [5] Other seed fell on rocky ground, where it did not have much soil, and immediately it sprang up, since it had no depth of soil. [6] And	And when a great crowd was gathering and people from town after town came to him, he said in a parable: [5] "A sower went out to sow his seed. And as he sowed, some fell along the path and was trampled underfoot, and the birds of the air devoured it. [6] And some fell on the rock, and as it grew up, it withered away, because it had no moisture. [7] And some fell among thorns, and the thorns grew up with it and choked it. [8] And some fell into good soil and grew and yielded a hundredfold." As he said these things, he called

soil, [6] but <u>when the sun rose they were scorched.</u> And <u>since they had no root,</u> they withered away. [7] Other seeds fell among thorns, and the thorns grew up and choked them. [8] Other seeds fell on good soil <u>and produced grain,</u> some a hundred-fold, <u>some sixty, some thirty.</u> [9] He who has ears, let him hear." [10] Then <u>the disciples</u> came and said to him, <u>"Why do you speak to them in parables?"</u> [11] And he answered them, "To you it has been given to know the secrets of the king-dom of heaven, but <u>to them it has not been given.</u> [12] <u>For to the one who has, more will be given, and he will have an abundance, but from the one who has not, even what he has will be taken away.</u> [13] <u>This is why I speak to them in parables, because seeing they do not see, and hearing they do not hear, nor do they understand.</u> [14] <u>Indeed, in their case the prophecy of Isaiah is fulfilled that says: "'You will indeed hear but never understand, and you will indeed see but never perceive.</u> [15] For this

when the sun rose, it was scorched, and since it had no root, it withered away. [7] Other seed fell among thorns, and the thorns grew up and choked it, <u>and it yielded no grain.</u> [8] And other seeds fell into good soil <u>and produced grain,</u> growing up and increasing and yielding <u>thirtyfold and sixtyfold</u> and a hundredfold." [9] And he said, "He who has ears to hear, let him hear." [10] And when he was alone, <u>those around him with the twelve asked him about the parables.</u> [11] And he said to them, "To you has been given the secret of the kingdom of God, but <u>for those outside everything is in parables,</u> [12] so that "they may indeed see but not per-ceive, and may indeed hear but not understand, lest they should turn and be forgiven." [13] <u>And he said to them, "Do you not understand this parable? How then will you under-stand all the parables?</u> [14] The sower sows the word. [15] And these are the ones along the path, where the word is sown: when they hear, Satan immediately comes and

out, "He who has ears to hear, let him hear."[9] And _{when} <u>his disciples asked him what this parable meant,</u> [10] he said, "To you it has been given to know the secrets of the kingdom of God, but <u>for others they are in parables,</u> so that 'seeing they may not see, and hearing they may not understand.' [11] Now the parable is this: <u>The seed is the word of God.</u> [12] The ones along the path are those who have heard; then the devil comes and takes away the word from their hearts, <u>so that they may not believe and be saved.</u> [13] And the ones on the rock are those who, when they hear the word, receive it with joy. But these have no root; they believe for a while, and in time of testing fall away. [14] And as for what fell among the thorns, they are those who hear, but as they go on their way they are choked by the cares and riches and pleasures of life, and their fruit does not mature. [15] As for that in the good soil, they are those who, hearing the word, <u>hold it fast in an honest and good heart,</u> and bear fruit with patience.

people's heart has grown dull, and with their ears they can barely hear, and their eyes they have closed, lest they should see with their eyes and hear with their ears and understand with their heart and turn, and I would heal them.' [16] But blessed are your eyes, for they see, and your ears, for they hear. [17] For truly, I say to you, many prophets and righteous people longed to see what you see, and did not see it, and to hear what you hear, and did not hear it. [18] "Hear then the parable of the sower: [19] When anyone hears the word of the kingdom and does not understand it, the evil one comes and snatches away what has been sown in his heart. This is what was sown along the path. [20] As for what was sown on rocky ground, this is the one who hears the word and immediately receives it with joy, [21] yet he has no root in himself, but endures for a while, and when tribulation or persecution arises on account of the word, immediately he falls away. [22] As for

takes away the word that is sown in them. [16] And these are the ones sown on rocky ground: the ones who, when they hear the word, immediately receive it with joy. [17] And they have no root in themselves, but endure for a while; then, when tribulation or persecution arises on account of the word, immediately they fall away. [18] And others are the ones sown among thorns. They are those who hear the word, [19] but the cares of the world and the deceitfulness of riches and the desires for other things enter in and choke the word, and it proves unfruitful. [20] But those that were sown on the good soil are the ones who hear the word and accept it and bear fruit, thirtyfold and sixtyfold and a hundredfold."

what was sown among thorns, this is the one who hears the word, but the cares of the world and the deceitfulness of riches choke the word, and it proves unfruitful. [23] As for what was sown on good soil, this is the one who hears the word and understands it. He indeed bears fruit and yields, <u>in one case a hundredfold, in another sixty, and in another thirty</u>."		

1.

THE PARABLE FOR TODAY

The true function of a preacher is to disturb the comfortable and to comfort the disturbed.

Chad Walsh, *Campus Gods on Trial* (cited by John Stott, *I Believe in Preaching*)

The parable of the sower is very well-known. So well-known in fact, that some may have turned from the book, thinking "Not the parable of the sower again!" When, however, we consider it in context—the context of our day (in this chapter) and of the Scriptures (in chapters two and three)—we begin to recover its original force. Not only does the parable call the church to forsake her immature or carnal (mis)perceptions of what makes a ministry successful, it challenges us to the core as to whether we are authentically Christian (which is to say, true followers of Jesus). Vocationally, then, the parable indicts much of what goes today for preaching, and, spiritually, it exposes the confusion of a pseudo-Christianity for the real thing.

Since you have taken up the book, I presume that the parable is not so familiar to you that it has bred contempt, or, that there is something about it which entices you to study it again. Regardless, you would do well not to presume that the book offers some light and easy reading. Jesus does not do bland. He wants us to sit up and to pay attention to his concerns, so much so that any study of his parable claiming to reflect his thought must, to some degree, have the same effect.

THE PARABLE IS FOR PREACHERS TODAY

Preachers, like anyone else, need to listen to preaching, and to Jesus' preaching above all. We come not only in different shapes and sizes, differing approaches and styles, but also nowadays with

1

the branding of a success or a flop. Jesus' parable, however, is the very antithesis of such categorizations of our celebrity culture and implicitly forewarns us, to draw more explicitly from Paul, that some successes will not appear so endowed once God has tried our work by fire, and some deemed flops and dismissed in this life will be rewarded (1 Corinthians 3:10-15).

In preparing us for the revolutionary character of Jesus' thinking, it is fitting to begin with a word to blue-eyed preachers and to those deemed to have bombed.

A word to popular preachers.

The parable is a caution from our Lord not to make too much of numbers. While preaching assumes there will be those to hear us, Christ warns us that a carnal, success-driven approach to ministry is contrary to the priority his Father places on committed discipleship. Jesus says to us in effect, "Who cares for the size of your crowds, if, at the end of the day, they don't enter my heavenly kingdom and live subject to my beneficent rule!" But Jesus does more than speak to us. He modeled for us a disregard for numbers.

Now we may agree with him in principle and yet succumb to the prevailing culture which idolizes success. There are telltale signs. Think of the minister who has fallen into the spirit of Diotrephes. Diotrephes, lamented the apostle John, loved preeminence among men (3 John 9-10). Yet, his spirit remains alive today. It does so, where:

- We have to be front and center of our ministries, expecting our names to be blasted everywhere and always with top billing.
- We believe other ministries exist for the sake of ours, and not ours for the sake of other ministries.

In such cases, there is a real danger of us setting up rivals to Christ's kingdom. At that point, our endeavors become not only sinful, but futile, for our kingdoms are doomed to fail. Look at church history. It is littered with the remains and the lessons of one grand church or ministry after another. Some faithfully fulfilled their particular calling, while others got too big for their britches and were brought down. Whether in church or state, there is only one eternal kingdom, the kingdom of heaven, and only one supreme King, the Lord Jesus Christ. Paradoxically, Christ who could have boasted of himself and his ministry, did not. Nor must we.

It is for each of us, then, to humble ourselves before our Lord and to esteem other faithful ministers and ministries as better than ourselves and our own. This is likely a more painful adjustment for some than for others, depending on how strongly we feel the lure of the crowd. Yet, faithful ministers embrace the cost, resonating the spirit of John the Baptist: "He must increase, but I must decrease" (John 3:30 [cf., Matthew 3:1-17; Mark 1:1-11; Luke 3:1-22; John 1:6-8, 19-42]). Ironically, only in the combination of self-abnegation and Christ-exaltation can true joy in ministry be found and sustained. It is fed, ultimately, not by professions of faith but by the influencing and observing of ongoing, maturing discipleship to Christ. This is not to deny that there is rejoicing in heaven and earth when a sinner turns back to God (Luke 15:7), but it is to claim that the joy is more than a momentary ecstasy. Rather, it is a delight that matures as the evidence of the turning accumulates.

If, then, we are in revolt against the will of Christ that we should maximize attention to ongoing disciple-making, then the parable of the sower will make for uncomfortable reading. What God is looking for, Christ says in his parable, are ministers and ministries preoccupied with ever increasing faithfulness to the Word and to God's vision of extending Christ's reign over hearts and lives.

Even where, however, ministers are of a mind to resist the allurements of the celebrity culture, success-oriented leaderships or congregations, affected even unknowingly by the culture, will evaluate our ministries by an exclusive obsession with numbers. The obsession gives birth to a need for instant gratification, which, in turn, creates an ethos which exalts the consumer above the will of God, and replaces principle with pragmatism as a way of meeting consumer demands.

Under such circumstances, a local church starts resembling a soccer club in which the minister of the Word becomes akin to a contracted club manager. If the points are not on the board, then no matter his diligence in prayer and study of the Word, he must be fired and another appointed. Such pressure can so wear on a preacher as to tempt him into craving popularity at the expense of a rigorous faithfulness to the Word. Giving people what they want rather than what they need, is, in the consumerist climate, his job security.

Such churches likely discover what many a struggling soccer club comes to realize, that the problem may not lie with the manager. They change the manager, but the team is relegated all the same. Instead of reviewing the state of the entire club, the leadership (typically under the sway of a few movers and shakers) sloppily assumes the manager is to blame. In clubs that are toxic, financial irresponsibility is ignored, as are their out-of-date training methods, or the string of player injuries. Thus, a change of manager makes little difference. Indeed, the change may further destabilize the club, hastening its downward spiral. Yet, if the soccer club is healthy but the results are poor, then that's another matter. A change of manager with a different style and relationship to the players may save the club from relegation.

Ministers of the Word, it must be said though, are not managers, and congregations are not soccer supporters. While doing business-like things, churches are not businesses as are soccer clubs. The results are ultimately out of the minister's hands. They are supremely in the hands of God, and, secondarily, in the hands of those who hear the Word preached. Note, as regards the parable of the sower, that our Lord explains the success of the sower (or otherwise) by analyzing the soil on which the seed of the Word falls *hul*, rather than by analyzing the sower. This is not to say that the sower of the seed bears no responsibility for his sowing, but it is to say that at the juncture in Jesus' ministry in which he discerns the need to preach in parables, his concern was to sift out his insincere listeners from those ready to receive him as their King. Now how many preachers would set in motion as our Lord did a plan to do that? And to do it at the height of their popularity? And how many leaderships and congregants would have the spiritual maturity to allow them to?

As familiar, then, as is the parable of the sower, it bears repeating in the context of the present. Attempts by preachers today to draw crowds other than by the unabashed proclamation of the word of the kingdom, and by hearers to coerce preachers into offering them self-centered consumerism rather than the proclamation of God's glory in and through the gospel, make the parable of the sower both timely and poignant. When, in the temple, "all cry, 'Glory!'" (Psalm 29:9) it is the glory of God and not of man which is to be front and center. The parable thus calls those of us who preach to submit our persons and our work to the reign of Christ.

It is, in effect, a particular call to us to repent if we have been bringing the world into the church. The word of the Lord through Joel jives with the parable of the sower:

> Be ashamed, O tillers of the soil; wail, O vinedressers, for the wheat and the barley, because the harvest of the field has perished. The vine dries up; the fig tree languishes. Pomegranate, palm, and apple, all the trees of the field are dried up, and gladness dries up from the children of man. Put on sackcloth and lament, O priests; wail, O ministers of the altar. Go in, pass the night in sackcloth, O ministers of my God! . . . Consecrate a fast; call a solemn assembly. Gather the elders and

all the inhabitants of the land to the house of the LORD your
God, and cry out to the LORD (Joel 1:11-13a, 14.)

Wherever ministry has become a man-centered, Word-disregarding, success-oriented carnality, the call to repentance is relevant. Our churches may have all the "bums on seats" we dreamed of during our seminary days, but if there is not the fruit of true Christian discipleship among our hearers, then our congregations are withering even as we boast of her numbers. Writes David Platt, "We can easily deceive ourselves, mistaking the presence of physical bodies in a crowd for the existence of spiritual life in a community."[1]

One evidence, at least locally, of the need of a return to the Lord is that church leaders are too often the last ones to support gatherings of prayer established to beseech God to visit his church.[2] This is not only detrimental to the spiritual health of the leader but is feasibly a dereliction of his leadership. A lesson from seminary days comes to mind, namely, that ninety per cent of our congregants will not rise higher in the things of God than we do as leaders. When congregants resist coming to prayer, stating explicitly, whether disingenuously or not, that they will start attending once the officebearers do, you know that the matter of leadership example is a live issue. All the more so, when you think of the role of ministers, elders, and deacons, as the chief repenters of the church. Where that sense of responsibility is missing, as also the intent of leading God's people in repenting, then the knock-on effect on the congregation is

---

[1] David Platt, *Radical: Taking Back Your Faith from the American Dream* (Colorado Springs, CO: Multnomah Books, 2010), 50.

[2] Part of this may be tradition wherein ministers, elders, and deacons are understood to do the work and the people to do the praying. The local ministry, *The Grand Awakening* (http://www.grandawakening.org/) rightly understands that if revival and awakening is going to come to West Michigan then the visible leadership of church leaders in public prayer is vital.

certain. States the adage, "As the leadership goes, so goes the church."

A word to discouraged preachers.

The parable of the sower offers, by contrast, a great tonic for those preachers who are not followed by great crowds but whose ministries expound God's Word, glorify his name, exalt Christ, depend on the Spirit, and fixate on walking souls from unbelief and impenitence through to a mature commitment to holiness of life. The parable makes the offer by rowing us against the current preoccupation with gathering masses, reminding us that God is more impressed by a committed proclamation of his revealed truth no matter the results than by seismic gatherings assembled through the trimming or contravening of God's Word and its application.

Faithfulness to God's Word and its true proclamation must, accordingly, be our main concern. We leave the numbers to God. They are nice, no one disputes that, but our worth as preachers is gauged not by how many pack into our churches, conference centers, and stadia, or even by how many "made decisions for Christ" (the converts), but by whether we have handled, applied, and prayed over the Word preached, proceeding from there to apply it on ground level to the people we serve. Through such a process lies the path to the making of authentic lifelong disciples of Christ (cf., Matthew 28:19).

Ministry that is Word-saturated and faithfully, boldly, but lovingly applied is the need of the hour. Observes John De Vries, "The Bible remains a best seller in the United States, but it is seldom read, in spite of the fact that over 80% of the homes in the United States have at least one copy."[3] With the plethora of study Bibles available for those who can afford them, and with cheap editions

---

[3] John De Vries, *God's Mission Vision: Pray, Go, Sow, Grow Love* (Grand Rapids: Ephesians 3:20 Publishing, 2018), 37.

given away by publishers, the Gideons, and outreach ministries, there is no excuse for this. The failure to read the Scriptures is a heart issue.

With comparatively few inclined to digest them, the temptation to abandon the Word in pulpit ministry is strong. Reaching people with the Scriptures is an uphill task. Signs of what the Word is accomplishing among those it reaches can be few and far between. Many a faithful minister strains his eyes in search of indications of God's transformation of his hearers. He must resist the temptation to exaggerate those discerned, or to use a misleading yardstick to procure a falsely positive assessment. Conversely, though, he must also push back against discouragement. States John Stott, "The occupational hazard of the Christian ministry and evangelism is discouragement."[4] If not faced down, discouragement quickly spirals us downward into cynicism and indifference to the modest outcomes perceived in this proverbial "day of small things" (Zechariah 4:10). When that happens, we exacerbate the problem, for to deny God's ongoing activity in and through the means he has ordained is to grieve the very Spirit we need to enliven us.

How to push back discouragement from our minds and hearts is often the question which besets ministers. By its very nature discouragement seems heavy and can feel immovable. What is more, the discouraged preacher may feel unable to make observations from his own pulpit without coming across as bitter or down on the congregation. Permit me, then, to make them here on his behalf, for to battle discouragement successfully we need a safe platform from which to strategize how to do so.

First, we are to *be proactive*. We counter discouragement—ideally, before it sets in—by preaching from time-to-time on the nature of preaching. Generally, this is best done amid an ongoing

---

[4] Quoted in *Gathered Gold: A Treasury of Quotations for Christians*, compiled by John Blanchard (Welwyn, Hertfordshire, England: Evangelical Press, 1984), 245.

series, where the passage or book naturally leads us to consider the subject. By letting loose the Word to govern the understanding and expectation of preaching, we implicitly encourage worthy estimates of the ministry of the Word and discourage those which are erroneous or carnal. In the process, we remind ourselves of our responsibility to rightly handle the Word of truth and the congregants of theirs to support us in prioritizing the Word. Jesus' parable does exactly that, as has the church at her best.

Today's spiritually anemic fare in public worship of addresses in self-help, and musical entertainment hard to distinguish from that of the world, compares negatively to the ministry of the church at her most powerful and influential. It is the preaching of the Word that has sustained the church down to the present. Thus, current fads in worship which downplay preaching would not only have been alien and anathema to Jesus, the apostles, the reformers, and the most notably used of God in history, they threaten to cut the church adrift from the very means God has used to establish and to spread his people across both time and space.

Faced with these stubborn facts, we await the fruit to come from the preached Word. It comes in God's timing and in God's way. Yes, we are to assemble hearers—the Hebrew for "preacher," *Qoheleth*, comes from the root *qahal* ("to assemble")—but when they come and how they come is ultimately a matter for God's Spirit (Psalm 110:3 [KJV]). As the parable of the sower teaches us, the Word is to be sown come what may. We preach it not in me-centered soundbites or eisegesis (verses ripped from their context), nor even in the dogmatic construal and Scripture-rivaling preaching of otherwise excellent catechetical summaries of the Word, but through the exposition and application of verses, passages, and books on their own terms. We preach them within the context of the overall revealed counsel of God (Acts 20:27), giving ourselves to the ministry of the Word and to prayer, as was the apostolic practice (Acts 6:4).

We take heart, then, from Dietrich Bonhoeffer's claim, that, "Neither failure nor hostility can weaken the messenger's conviction that he has been sent by Jesus."[5] The word of the kingdom we preach does, in God's timing, glorify him, save souls, transform people, heal churches, and spread the kingdom. The Lord's wheels grind slowly outside of revival, but they grind surely. Therefore, we preach in season and out of it (2 Timothy 4:2), for faithful ministers are joined at the hip to the Word. To abandon its proclamation because the Word is out of favor not only contravenes Scripture, it perpetuates its neglect. Just as our stomachs shrink with a declining appetite for food, so our ability to take in and to digest the Word regresses the more we neglect the Word.

Second, we are to *be realistic*. Whereas the cynic thinks in his deeply rutted discouragement that everything about ministry is of no use and that there is no alternative but to throw in the towel, the realist accepts that there will be setbacks in ministry and that God is at work notwithstanding them. His thinking is governed not by the discouragements which come his way, but by Jesus' view of ministry. Our Lord has promised that the Word shall have the effect God wills for it and that, before the throne of God, we shall be able to see this more clearly than we can at present. Then and only then will we know how much God has been accomplishing behind the scenes. We are thus led not by our present discouragements but by our desire to see the smile of our Lord and his pronouncement over us: "Well done, good and faithful servant"! (Matthew 25:23).

Third, we must *be discerning*. After all, discouragement can be distorting and does not lend itself to a balanced assessment of our ministries. A maturing experience of pulpit ministry helps us in this regard, for years of reflecting on the feedback of our hearers teaches us that:

---

[5] Dietrich Bonhoeffer, *The Cost of Discipleship*, Revised and unabridged edition containing material not previously translated (New York: MacMillan Publishing Co., Inc., 1963), 236.

- Encouraging feedback may be sincere, but it may also amount to nothing more than flattery. We welcome it, of course, while yet guarding ourselves against pride on the one hand and the gut-wrenching disappointment of the false profession of faith or the unfulfilled promise of growth on the other. Time tells the sincerity or otherwise of the feedback.

- Criticism can be discouraging, even devastating, but it may also reveal our faithfulness to God's Word. After all, the truth is not always palatable to our hearers. The carnal, immature, or backslidden ordinarily prefer, for the sake of appearances, to criticize the preacher than God's Word. Preachers can be, and often are, scapegoats for some gripe against God, his Word, or his church. Once we realize this, the criticism can become strangely encouraging. It reveals that the Word is being understood and that hearts are being touched, contrary to what the feedback initially suggests. In such scenarios the criticism is a backhanded complimenting of our faithfulness. It takes, though, godly, informed counsel to help us to deduce when the source of the criticism diminishes or nullifies the criticism made.

- God rules and overrules in all the feedback, whether positive or negative. We recall that the Word is a savor of death unto death as well as of life unto life (2 Corinthians 2:16). Naturally, we desire the success of the apostle Paul (?–67?), of George Whitefield (1714–1770), or of Charles Haddon Spurgeon (1834–1892), but many of us must settle for the immediately unforeseeable fruit of a Noah, an Isaiah, a Jesus, a William Carey ("My only genius is that I can plod"), and a host of others who sowed the Word but saw little fruit come from it, at least during their lifetimes.

After a hundred years of preaching, Noah entered the ark with but his family (Genesis 7:7; 1 Peter 3:20). Isaiah was directed to preach until just a tenth of the people remained (today, he would be fired long before completing the Lord's call!). Even Jesus' ministry might come into question, for whereas he was once followed by thousands, by the end of his three years of ministry throughout the land there were but 120 followers left in Jerusalem (in the south) and another 500 in Galilee (to the north).[6] That sort of hemorrhaging over the course of three years would nowadays result in many a church calling for "a change at the top." After all, the bigger the Christian industry complex becomes the greater the temptation to put financial considerations before the countercultural dynamics of the kingdom.

Not only, then, does criticism of ministries ordained to be a savor of death unto death reveal gross ignorance of the Word, it forgets that before long Jesus' smaller, fearful band of disciples was empowered by the knowledge of his resurrection and by the fullness of the Spirit to turn the world upside down (Acts 17:6). The fact that this turnaround was promised by Christ, but unforeseen by his apostles, ought to give trigger-happy church leaderships some pause for thought.[7] Before so fretting as to fire the faithful minister of the Word or to pressurize him into moving on, church leaders would do well to reflect on whether they are going ahead of God and his timetable for the growth he has promised to come from his Word. If the imperishable seed of the Word is being planted, then give it time to bear fruit in souls converted, matured, and commissioned for service.

---

[6] Acts 1:15; 1 Corinthians 15:6.
[7] For more on the turnaround, see the Afterword.

Fourth, it will help us to *be self-examining*. Although a treatment of the parable of the sower is not the place for a critique of preaching, since that is not the point of it, we are to ensure that no part of our discouragement is self-inflicted. This entails asking ourselves some searching questions. For example, whether our preaching is boring. Tedious ministries have either been sapped of their vitality by the lifelessness and lukewarmness of their congregational contexts (in which instances it would be better for ministers to safeguard their zeal by moving on to more promising pastures), or they have by their sluggishness created the apathy of the congregation (which needs to be addressed while there is still energy and vision to do so). Neither scenario can legitimately claim that the parable of the sower justifies the way things are, for true commitment to the Word is not only theoretical but spiritual. A genuine proclamation and application of the Word possesses a loftiness of vision and energy in both the pulpit and pews. It is not languid but full of verve.

Nor should our preaching be esoteric, or out of reach of those interested in the Word. A preacher may preach with a high view of Scripture and a high use of it, while yet blurring the hearer's access to the gospel. Observed Bonhoeffer in the 1930s: "It is just not true that every word of criticism directed against contemporary preaching is a deliberate rejection of Christ and proceeds from the spirit of Antichrist. So many people come to church with a genuine desire to hear what we have to say, yet they are always going back home with the uncomfortable feeling that we are making it too difficult for them to come to Jesus."[8] Rather, our preaching must be clear and sensitive to the sociocultural context of our hearers. The same God who sovereignly decrees the impact of our ministries, has included within his plan our responsibility to read our hearers as well as his Word. This does not mean that we are called to be

---

[8] Bonhoeffer, *The Cost of Discipleship*, 38.

showmen or comedians, or that we are to think that transient Twitter followers, cost-free Facebook likes, or even professions of conversion guarantee faithful communication of the gospel. Nevertheless, the prophets, Christ, and the apostles did succeed in combining homiletical methods and gospel messages to address effectively the needs of the day. They teach us that if our gospel-soaked expositions of the Word are not reaching the people before us, then however biblical our content we are not preaching. It is Christ and his cross then, and not me and my foibles, which are the legitimate offences of ministry. Accordingly, to avoid discouragement we must embrace "truth in the inward being" (Psalm 51:6), appealing to the parable of the sower for support of our ministries only where it is appropriate to do so.

Fifth, having checked our methods and message and made the necessary adjustments, we are to *be compassionate.* Some hearers need pity—no, prayer! Think of those who continually respond to us with the lament as old as the hills: "I don't get anything out of the preaching!" The claim is in clear contradiction of the promise of the Lord:

> As the rain and snow come down from heaven and do not return there but water the earth, making it bring forth and sprout, giving seed to the sower and bread to the eater, so shall my word be that goes out from my mouth; it shall not return to me empty, but it shall accomplish that which I purpose and shall succeed in the thing for which I sent it. (Isaiah 55:10-11)

While the hackneyed claim may be a euphemism for some other legitimate complaint against us, our ministries, or, as likely, the leadership or the church (in which case the plaintiff needs more honesty and to redirect the criticism), it is as possible that the complaint is true. For the habitual plaintiff, evading all personal responsibility for the way the Word is heard, may simply be dull of hearing, possessing a heart that is self-deceived. Such a person needs to be converted, matured by the transformative grace of God, or strengthened to resist the appeal of consumerism. Being pandered to by the church leadership can be counterproductive.

Sixth, to counter discouragement *be prayerful*. Naturally the minister, called of God to give himself to prayer and to the study of the Word, must be a praying and a prayerful man. The chief responsibility for countering his personal discouragement is his. Reflection on God's attributes, covenant, promises, and calling can invigorate his prayers afresh with faith and his ministry with renewed confidence. With the help of the Spirit, the man of God may pray himself back into a state of buoyancy, thereby outflanking the devil and his demons doing all in their power to disable God's servant.

That said, a congregation may play a vital role in ministering to the minister of the Word. Not simply by telling him that they are praying for him and his effectiveness in ministry, but by revealing their hearts for him in prayer within his hearing. To minister to a people and to rarely hear them pray for you or for the Word you preach is deeply troubling. They may love you in a whole host of ways, but if they do not love you enough to pray for you in your presence, they understand neither your greatest need nor the spiritual battle you face in getting the Word to them.

It is, though, not simply corporate prayer that is needed in church life, but a certain type of it. God's people do well when they selflessly balance maintenance prayer (concerning pregnancies, sicknesses and affliction, bereavements, and the like) and frontline prayer (concerning the ministry of the Word, the spread of the kingdom, the aiding of missionaries and the persecuted). Such communal times of prayer for the growth of the kingdom are sorely lacking. While different churches and theological traditions have their particular practices and cultures, there is, it seems to me, something to the old fundamentalist adage, "You can tell how many people love the church by how many turn up on Sunday morning;

how many love the minister by how many turn up on Sunday evening; and how many love Jesus by how many turn up at the prayer meeting." Why might there be some truth in this? Because, as A.W. Tozer is said to have observed, the prayer meeting is the only meeting in the life of the church where God is the sole entertainment. Additionally, Spurgeon, I believe it was, referred to the prayer meeting as the engine room of the church.

Whether we agree with all this or not, the need in many places for fresh spiritual power on the ministry of the Word is indisputable. To extrapolate for a moment from the parable of the sower, we need the heavens to open and the water of God's Spirit to pour afresh on the seed sown in the heart. As things stand, it is difficult to tell whether consumerist attacks on the minister of the Word are grieving the Spirit and, therefore, hinder the revival of the church; or whether the fresh reviving of God's Spirit, for which an increasing number in formerly Christianized lands are praying, will convict God's people of having taken his faithful servants for granted. Regardless, there is much sin present where ministers of the Word hear the criticisms from their people, but not their hearts poured out before the Lord in interceding for his ministry of the Word.

We can go further. The very toxicity which produces such negativity in church life likely explains, at least in part, why visitors do not return and why more members do not serve in such churches. Ironically, the very people decrying the pastor most for not being more successful in enlarging the church, contribute significantly to the undermining of his effectiveness. It is worth remembering that in postmodernity those looking for a church to join consider not only "the authority figure" who stands at the front each week (in regard to whom they may be somewhat cynical), but the authenticity of the congregation. When visitors sit in the back rows, overhearing the muttering and murmuring that sometimes goes on there, you can be sure they will not be visiting for long.

There is, then, a correlative relationship between prayer for the ministry of the Word and criticism of it. Where the one is present the other evaporates. Where the latter becomes the norm, you can presume that the prayer meetings of the church are empty or nonexistent. We cannot bless God for his servant and, simultaneously, cut him down with our tongues. Let me reword that. We can do and do so, but Scripture clearly tells us that we ought not to (James 3:9-10), and that to do so is sin.

THE PARABLE IS FOR HEARERS

The parable is described by Jesus as the parable of the sower (Matthew 13:18) and yet, paradoxically, it focuses on the soil on which the seed lands. It is fitting, then, that we should reflect on the hearing of the Word today. I think especially of the current drifting away from the hearing of the Word. Some once attending morning and evening worship now attend but the once, and some once attending but a single service on the Lord's Day now attend but several times a month. Some once attending but periodically are denouncing the faith, so much so that books are being published to document and to offset the trends.[9]

Many do not want to leave behind the Christian faith altogether, so they opt for congregations with fewer expectations about worship and service, and, because of their size, with less accountability for their attendance. Thus, the church which appears highly successful on the surface of things, might not be quite so stellar when considered in terms of discipleship. Conversely, what may appear to be a flop when measured in terms of numbers may, in

---

[9] See, for instance, David Kinnaman's *unChristian: What a New Generation Really Thinks About Christianity* (Grand Rapids: Baker Books, 2007); Julia Dunn's *Quitting Church: Why the Faithful Are Fleeing and What to Do about It* (Grand Rapids: Baker Books, 2008); and *Already Gone: Why Your Kids Will Quit Church and What You Can Do to Stop It* by Ken Ham and Britt Beemer (Green Forest, AR: Master Books, 2009).

fact, be doing very well in fulfilling God's desire for making solid and reliable disciples.

Suffice it to say that there is great need for us today to check our hearts. Leaving aside the churches which have a history of starving the people of God's Word and which, long ago, ceased to be true churches, we need go no further than the biblically orthodox to observe that the means of grace and the hearing of the Word are not generally valued as once they were. Many churches are plateauing, the very existence of others is under threat, and too many to count are already closed.

A word to drifting hearers.

The idea of the Lord's people drifting is not easy to depict, for it involves a mix of that which is outrightly sinful and that which is but unhelpful. Scripture, though, tells us to lay aside not only the sins that cling so closely to us but the weights as well (Hebrews 12:1). That is to say, the things that not only are outwardly opposed to God's will but also those matters which in themselves are lawful but which may hinder our personal spiritual growth.

The use of the Lord's Day is a good case to consider in this regard; both because it is the primary day for the preaching and hearing of the Word, and because it has increasingly suffered neglect and is prone to both sinful and unhelpful usage.

This claim is based, first, on the historic interpretation of Scripture which views the Lord's Day to be an apostolic outworking of the fourth commandment: "Remember [or "Observe"] the Sabbath day, to keep it holy" (Exodus 20:8; Deuteronomy 5:12). The apostles retained the divine dedication of one day in seven for his worship and service but were led to alter the day from the last to the first day of the week. The change signified the unsurpassed relevance and victory of the resurrection of Jesus from the dead (Revelation 1:10), and teaches us the abiding authority of the moral law and of Christ's Lordship over his day.[10] Thus, we dare not dismiss the use of the Lord's Day as a gray area of the Christian life, although, admittedly, there are areas of its use which are left to our consciences.

Many, in letting slip the importance of a Sabbath to honor God and to invest in his work, are doubtless reacting against a prior legalistic distortion of the Sabbath principle. In the worst cases, Sabbath-keeping became tantamount to a means of salvation. In less severe cases, the Sabbath principle was upheld with a myriad of expectations more akin to the days of the old covenant. Yet, the overreaction against the distortion of the principle and the self-justification the legalism has provided, serves, in my view, to promote sin. It does so by disregarding the moral law, by pandering to the flesh in the abandonment of public worship, and thus weakens the witness of the church.

What is needed is a true or nonlegalistic Sabbatarianism which deems the day a delight rather than a drudgery. We mark it not in the fear of the church under age (although even then in Old Testament times God's people were charged with calling the Sabbath a delight [Isaiah 58:13]), but in the fuller joy of the church come of age now that Christ and the Spirit have been given to us (Galatians 3:23–4:7).

Three historical factors explain this joy. In a Christian Sabbatarianism:

- *There is far less emphasis on strictures and penalties.* The church come of age, standing on the shoulders of our forebears, now knows that one day in the week, as directed or determined by God, is to be dedicated to his worship and

---

[10] For more on the legal distinctions of moral, judicial, and ceremonial law, see chap. 2.

service, and that obedience to such a principle is precious to God and beneficial to ourselves. God, therefore, has no more need of belaboring the strictures and penalties first given to Israel (the church under age) than a parent has of continuing to lay down the law to a child now grown up ("Brush your teeth!"; "Put your coat on!"; "Tie up your shoe laces!"; and so forth). The rules still apply, but once they are learned the emphasizing of them ceases.

- *There are far fewer strictures and penalties.* We need to distinguish the moral law which is abiding from the judicial and ceremonial laws which, respectively, have ended and been fulfilled. Accordingly, those strictures and penalties related to the judicial and/or ceremonial law of Israel are also no more (e.g., the penalties for picking up sticks on the Sabbath [Numbers 15:32-35]). Thus, there is under the Christian Sabbath a greater liberty to decide those pertinent issues left undetermined by the moral law, and in an age that raises issues unforeseen in the days of Moses (e.g., whether rest for worship and service permits recreational sports and the use of media).

- *There is more emphasis on Christ and the gospel.* Israelites looked forward in faith to the Christ who was to come. They saw him in sacrifices, ceremonies, and festivals which were divinely ordained and designed for that very purpose. In effect, the Mosaic Sabbath was top-down (by law). We, however, look back to a Christ who is to come. The governance of the Christian Sabbath, while yet top down (according to the moral law and applied by the Holy Spirit sent from heaven), possesses a measure of self-governance. We have been given the Holy Spirit who works in our hearts so that we do freely from our new natures what is pleasing to God. The Spirit still guides us by means of the moral law, but in this new covenant era the Christian is more conscious of the loving guidance of the Spirit than of the demands of the law. God the Son impresses on us through the ministry of God the Spirit that the (Christian) Sabbath is a delightful and necessary gift to us from God the Father. Thus, we embrace each Lord's Day the access to the Father that Christ has purchased for us on the cross and that the Spirit empowers us to use through his renewal of our natures. In these new natures we rejoice in the victory we have through Christ's resurrection, looking forward in confidence to the eternal rest to come.

The claim that the Lord's Day can be put to unhelpful or sinful uses is supported not only by biblical principle but, second, and following on, by the ministry of the Spirit. The Spirit reminds us not only that the worshipful and service-oriented use of the Christian Sabbath brings glory to God, but that it liberates us from the bondage of a nonstop workweek and from the emptiness of inordinate (that is to say, self-centered or self-serving) pleasure. The Lord's Day is the space in the week that God has created for nurturing our communion with him. The more we safeguard that space and the time it gives us, the more we find delight on the day in the living God. It is, then, not only for God's glory but for our benefit that we invest spiritually in the day.

To aid us in this, God structures our freedom in Christ around his directive to be in the assembly of the Lord's people each Lord's Day, worshiping God and provoking one another to love and good works (Hebrews 10:24-25). We thus resist all temptations to be absent from worship, and, as parents, do all we can to avoid introducing children to the practice of skipping worship.

For sure we have liberty of conscience to decide the details of the day outside of worship services, but we decide them as those brought by Christ into an era of spiritual maturity and in light of our voluntary submission to the reign of Christ and to the leading of the

Spirit. We thus consider activities not covered by the Word in terms of whether they help us or hinder us from glorifying God on his day and from honoring Christ and serving his cause.

If you are a new Christian or have let the Lord's Day slip, the thought of dedicating or rededicating the Lord's Day to the Lord may appear narrow. Yet, as Christians, baptized at conversion with the Spirit and filled repeatedly with him (cf., Acts 4:31 and Ephesians 5:18), the command to honor the Lord's Day is not burdensome (1 John 5:3), nor is it truncated by the termination of evening services. We either request the recommencement of evening worship, look for an evening worship service to attend, or find ways on Sunday evenings to serve the kingdom pastorally, evangelistically, or practically (as in works of necessity or mercy).

Clearly, the liberty of conscience we have with regard to the details of the day is not to become a foil for unrighteousness (Galatians 5:13; 1 Peter 2:16). Nor is the liberty to be used in non-sinful but unhelpful ways which dull our senses to the privilege and experience of communion with God. To think that by playing fast and loose with the Lord's Day we increase our joy, is foolhardy. The more the day becomes about us rather than about God the drier our souls become. We may succeed in suppressing our guilt in robbing God of his worship and of our investment in his cause, but sooner or later, if we are truly saved, we shall be brought to a place in which we resonate the sentiment of William Cowper (1731–1800):

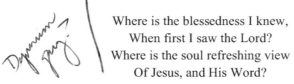

Where is the blessedness I knew,
When first I saw the Lord?
Where is the soul refreshing view
Of Jesus, and His Word?

We recover the profound joy of the Lord's Day not by substituting the neglect of the Lord's Day with a joyless legalism, but by returning to God, humbly asking him to restore unto us our first love for him and the joy of our salvation.

Ours is not the first generation in need of turning back from our laxities. Nineteenth-century missionary John G. Paton (1824–1907) complained of those who, like the heathen among whom he labored in the South Sea Islands, gave up manual labor on the day but utilized it too much in selfish pleasures, feasting, and drinking. Although Paton does not say so, I presume they neglected the means of grace to do so. Later he wrote, "When I returned to so-called civilization, and saw how the Lord's Day was abused in *white* Christendom, my soul longed after the holy Sabbaths of Aniwa!"[11] That said, the Lord's Day was generally better guarded in previous generations than it is today. Following one wave of revival after another, families overall had a greater sense of the reverence and privilege of worship, and thus factored into their plans the consecration of the day. We may criticize some of the ways they kept the day, but what would they think of us, having squandered our Judeo-Christian heritage by failing to safeguard the Lord's Day in society and by becoming party to its desecration.

Take, for instance, the realm of sport. My father, an avid tennis fan, whose father would have been in the first round of Wimbledon in the 1920s had he not lost the final of the army championship, told of how the Wimbledon final in 1972 was postponed from the Saturday to the Sunday because of rain. Stan Smith, a Christian, made it to the final, yet, according to what my father had read, was in a bind as to what to do. The final had never been held on Sunday before. From memory, Billy Graham warned Smith that if he went ahead and played, British Christians would not understand. The rest is history. Smith played. He beat Ile Nastase, but a golden opportunity was lost to make a stand against the rejection of the Lord's Day. It was a moment in history when a stand for principle could have counted.

---

[11] *John G. Paton: Missionary to the New Hebrides*, first published 1889; reprint ed. [Edinburgh and Carlisle, PA: The Banner of Truth Trust, 1994), 90, 380.

Nowadays, few blink at the thought of our Christian sporting heroes capitulating to employers, television companies, and to sponsors. Jürgen Klopp, the beloved manager of Liverpool Football Club, is sincere when he says he does not understand how life works without the Christian faith, yet he seems to have no conscience in pursuing trophies on the Lord's Day among an Anfield crowd there to worship the club rather than the Lord. In fairness, Klopp may be true to his Lutheran-influenced views of the Lord's Day, but it is puzzling that he seems to be untroubled by the sight of 40,000 plus fans attending the stadium instead of the church, chanting football lyrics for hymns, being entertained by the team rather than by the Word of God, and treating the club as God. Many other professing Christians share the same indifference to the idolatry indicated by the neglect of the Lord's Day. How can this be? Our apathy is a far cry from the paroxysm or fit Paul experienced when observing Athens full of idolatry (Acts 17:16).

Whatever God has planned in response to the abuse of his day, we can be certain in the meantime of the impact on the wider church of its high-profiled neglect. Christian celebrities have, it is to be feared, had more influence on the church's indifference to the reign of Christ over his day than on the public in leading idolaters to the living and written Word. Doubtless, there is much pressure on such celebrities, but this is largely because a united stand was not made by the church at the outset of the push for Sunday sport. Consequently, we are found today in the rather hypocritical position of lauding Eric Liddel of *Chariots of Fire* fame for not running in the heat on the Lord's Day at the 1924 Paris Olympics, while simultaneously giving passes to today's sporting heroes who desecrate the Lord's Day and offer tacit agreement to the masses in doing so.

Those of us of the Reformed tradition who tend to see ourselves as the guardian of the church's standards and have traditionally upheld the Lord's Day as sacred, are not averse to forgoing Christ's claim over his day. Few come out and revise their understanding of what the Scriptures teach concerning it or ask for an exception when subscribing to subordinate standards. Nevertheless, pragmatism rather than the will of Christ too often holds sway in a tradition of theology which has, historically, put a premium on principle. Sin in other ways and one can be marginalized for life, but succeed on the Lord's Day in the things that don't matter for eternity, encouraging others by our example to forgo worshiping God, and next to nothing is said!

Has there been to date as much as a question mark over Keith Reich, a former president of a Reformed seminary coaching in the NFL on the Lord's Day? In an age in which American football, like so many major sports, has reached the point of idolatry, did anyone question the propriety of our brother serving as the offensive coordinator of the Philadelphia Eagles on the Lord's Day in the 2017 Super Bowl LII? From all the reports Keith Reich is a wonderful man. He is orthodox in his theology and typifies a Reformed worldview appreciative of the value of the secular as well as the sacred.[12] But as a Reformed seminary president, Keith Reich would have subscribed to the Westminster Confession of Faith's summary of biblical teaching on the Lord's Day (WCF 21:7-8). It is possible that he obtained an exemption from his subscription, or changed his mind about the Sabbath principle after stepping down as president, but it is as likely that he typifies a drift within our Reformed tradition into pragmatism ("if it works, it must be right"). Increasingly, we seem to be picking and choosing our theological and moral outrage, depending on the celebrity ranking of the offender.

---

[12] See representative articles "NFL Coach Keith Reich Speaks Out on Faith and Work" (https://stream.org/nfl-coach-frank-reich-speaks-faith-work/), and "From Seminary President to NFL Head Coach," (www.thegospelcoalition.org/article/seminary-president-nfl-head-coach-indianapolis-colts-frank-reich/). Both articles were accessed on March 30, 2019.

Between our surrender of the Lord's Day to sport and to shopping (another ready-made example of capitulation), we are surely not surprised at all that attendance at worship and the consecration of the day have suffered, with many drifting away from hearing the Word. In this light, the parable of the sower, set in the context of the kingdom of heaven and the reign of Christ over his disciples, asks us some very searching questions. Far from being safe and familiar, the parable pointedly and powerfully calls us to examine our ways.

A word to concerned hearers.

Our turning back to God begins by taking seriously the evidences of the drift. We cannot simply declare, defensively, that former generations were legalists, and that we are the ones who have at last understood the freedom of the gospel. If this were the case, we would also be the ones turning the world upside down, beginning with the Western world. Rather, the world is, at least in the secularizing nations, doing everything possible to conform the church to its image.

Not all megachurches have brought the world into the church, but can there be any doubt that in seeking relevance many have crossed the line, becoming like the world in order to win the world? Many years ago, I recall looking down the aisle of a train, noticing a passenger facing my direction reading a secular magazine. The question on the front cover read: "Has the Church Hijacked Club Culture?" More broadly posed, we may ask, has the church hijacked the world? Now that question is relevant not only for this or that branch of the professing church, it is relevant for each of us personally. Have I, as representative of the church, coopted the ways of the world in my thinking, my speech, and my actions? Are there areas of my life from which I have willfully excluded Christ? If so, then I, too, have cause for repentance.

Speaking corporately, so do our congregations where the world has too much say—where congregants have become spectators of a weekly performance; are satisfied to breathe in Christianity-lite, free of the mind-blowing but life-inconveniencing truths of Scripture; and are disinterested in eldership oversight and the personal accountability arising from membership of a small group or church. In this light, we cannot be surprised that megachurches are supersizing, causing in America the churches of 500 or so to dwindle into smaller churches (while retaining their huge edifices), and the smaller community churches to struggle for their existence. Clearly, the need of corporate revival is equal to that of personal revival. Other than the return of Christ, the revival of the church is our most urgent need and the best guarantee we have of halting the drifting.

While many, being "at ease in Zion" (Amos 6:1), seem content for things to remain the way they are, there has been in recent years a marked increase of concern that God would revive his church. Currently, the focus is very much on what the world is doing with its movement toward secularism or neo-paganism and the amorality (immorality) of sexual ethics, gender identity, abortion (now borderline infanticide), and anticipated euthanasia. Yet, the repentance of God's people precedes that of society, just as the revival of the church precedes an awakening in the surrounding culture. It is pleasant to speak of the phenomena of revival, after all the idea of full churches feeds our desire to be or to follow celebrities, yet an authentic movement of God's Spirit entails a significant and heartbreaking purging of the church of her sins. Perhaps the tarrying of revival may be explained by our desire for the former but not the latter. We can haggle about the details of the Lord's Day, but this is surely one area in which we are called to retrace our steps.

While revival will, in one sense, halt the drift away from public worship and the consecrated use of the Lord's Day, in another sense revival will serve as a catalyst for another kind of drifting. Those having embraced a cushy cultural "Christianity" *in lieu* of the real thing, will, apart from repentance, exit the church, if they haven't already done so, once the claims of Christ as King and the costs of Christianity hit home under the fresh anointing of the preached Word. Unrepentant cultural "Christians" will quickly decide that Christianity is not for them after all. Thus revival, we anticipate, will herald simultaneously a movement to the center and to the fringes of church life. This is normative in church life, yet in revival the flow of incomers and outgoers is accentuated. Obviously, the records of revival and subsequent awakening disclose that there are more incomers than outgoers; nevertheless, the principle holds true: Revival both halts and occasions drifting. Genuine Christians seek once more to fulfill in love the duties of obedience outlined by God in his Word, false Christians threatened with exposure by the sheer power of the ministry of the Spirit make a run for it. Jesus' parable of the sower helps us to comprehend what we are and what we would do were God to revive his church once more.

As Christianity loses its social perks in the secularizing nations, so we are learning the difference between loosely associating with a Christian crowd (as so-called cultural "Christians" do) and earnestly following the Lord Jesus as his true disciples (as in biblical Christianity). We are all capable of wanting shorter and lighter me-centered sermons, a take-it or leave-it attitude to the Lord's Day, spare-change "tithing," a leave-it-to-others attitude toward service in the church, and a carelessness for the plight of the lost, but without the life of the Spirit within us, this is as much as the cultural "Christian" can offer to God. The cultural "Christian" seeks to do enough to cover the bases of Christianity, hoping to get close enough to Jesus to curry favor with him, but not so close as to hear his call to live under his reign. Cultural "Christians" have a mental respect for Christ but no heart of love to offer him and no readiness to surrender to him. The "Christianity" of the cultural "Christian" is an undisciplined, cost-free christianese. It turns out not to be the Christianity for which Christ lived and died. Not being genuine, it is false.

The authentic Christian by contrast, possessing the Spirit, grows in understanding and appreciation that:

- The glorification of God is the most important reason we gather for worship.
- The Lord's Day is for the Lord. We use it to rejoice in our resurrected Savior and to serve his purposes.
- There is a real and lasting joy in bringing on the first day of the week our tithes and offerings for the work of the gospel.
- We are to serve in Christ's church for her upbuilding and the reaching of those on the outside.

Often, we fall short of such biblical ideals, yet the lives of authentic Christians are marked by repentance for personal sin on the one hand and by a heavy-heartedness about today's drift on the other. We lament when cultural "Christians" prefer to merge back in with the world than to come to Christ, but we take consolation in the thought that with every defection of a cultural "Christian" the world gains a clearer picture from the combined witness of the church of what Christianity is really about.

Jesus uses his parable, then, for several purposes:

- *To press us to decide whether we are truly his.* If you find yourself realizing that cultural "Christianity" is all you have known, that it is not all it is cracked up to be, and that it is in fact not the Christianity Jesus taught, do stick with the study. Embrace the discomfort, for God is well able to meet with you in it. No one who has endured conviction of sin has ever regretted it. In God's good hand, it occasions faith in Christ, repentance toward God, and a consequent freedom from the bondage of sin.

29

- *To call his disciples to recover the implications of his kingship over their lives.* If we find ourselves away from Christ, claiming to be his but bucking his will for our lives, we must expect to be challenged by the parable. There is no harm in that discomfort either, for God uses his challenges to bring forth spiritual fruit in our lives.

- *And, finally, to encourage those hearers of his Word affirming their submission to him.* Jesus says to you in effect, "Keep on keeping on! It is your joy to do your Sovereign's will."

STUDY QUESTIONS: SESSION ONE

1. What characteristics would you list to distinguish a carnal from a spiritual approach to the preaching or teaching of the Word?

2. Churches do business-like things but are not businesses. Discuss how churches differ from businesses.

3. Discuss the erosion of the Lord's Day and its impact on attendance at worship and on the way we prepare for it. What are the causes and evidences of the erosion, and its solutions?

4. What else do you see today of a spiritual drift which ought to encourage the Christian church to repentance? Would you support your minister in so proclaiming and expounding God's Word on its own terms that he calls you to confess our drifting?

5. When and on what grounds should the claim "I don't get anything out of the preaching!" be challenged?

6. When is it right and wrong to be a) disturbed, b) comforted by the Word?

Prayer: Grant me, O Lord, a mind to see and a heart to lament the sins of your church, and a will to seek your face for her reviving. Begin that revival with me, so that the decisions I make may glorify your name, uphold your law, and exalt Christ, my Savior and King. Amen.

In preparation for chapter two, read: 2 Samuel 7:1-17; Acts 28:11-31.

PART ONE

"HEAR THEN THE PARABLE OF THE SOWER"

Matthew 13:18

2.

THE PARABLE AND THE KINGDOM

From that time Jesus began to preach, saying,
"Repent, for the kingdom of heaven is at
hand."

Matthew 4:17

By now you will have picked up how weighty is Jesus'
parable of the sower. It is far from trite—a watered down, overly
familiar, untroubling, and uninspiring "earthly story with a heavenly
meaning." Rather, Jesus has given both preachers and hearers of the
Word a gracious but firm challenge to seek afresh the face of God.
Since you are reading this, I presume you are up for it. Take heart,
no one loses out for humbly submitting to Jesus.

In entering our study proper we commence with the
important background of the parable and the parables at large.[1]
Since they are essentially parables *of the kingdom*, it behooves us to
possess an overall knowledge of what the Bible means by the
kingdom. This is a theme which you may often have encountered in
Scripture. Certainly, as a Briton it stands out to me because our
country has a monarchy. If you live in a republic, as most readers
do, the theme may pique your curiosity, since you likely have in
your nation a president for head of state rather than a king or a

---

[1] If you plan on studying the parables in their entirety, the parable of the sower is
an obvious place to begin, though not the only place. There are studies and
commentaries to walk you through them all. See the suggestions for further
reading at the rear of the book. Benjamin Keach, for instance, begins with eight
similitudes, since he includes them as parables due to their "use of natural things
by way of allusion or comparison, to open spiritual things, the better to our
understanding" (*Exposition of the Parables*, Series One, reprint ed. [Grand
Rapids: Kregel, 1991], 2). He then expounds four other allusions or comparisons,
labeling them as parables, although only one of them is explicitly labeled a
parable (Luke 5:36-37).

queen. We take our view of the kingdom, however, not from today's political systems (or even from those of extra-biblical history), but from Scripture. The theme is mentioned in both Testaments and in various contexts and is so rich that we need to be clear as to what we refer to when mentioning it in relation to the parable of the sower.

UNDERSTAND THE KINGDOM

The Scriptures speak of the kingdom in two ways, as the universal rule of God over the cosmos and as the saving rule of Jesus Christ on earth.

The universal rule of God.

When Scripture refers to God's sovereign rule over heaven and earth in their entirety, it refers to God's self-assertion over all his works: creation, providence, and redemption. Nothing and no one is outside of God's reign over his universe.[2] In this sense, the theme of kingdom is more all-encompassing than even the theme of covenant and is either assumed or explicitly mentioned throughout Scripture.

God's universal reign is mentioned periodically throughout the Old Testament. Consider 1 Chronicles 29:11:

> Yours, O LORD, is the greatness and the power and the glory
> and the victory and the majesty, for all that is in the heavens and
> in the earth is yours. Yours is the kingdom, O LORD, and you
> are exalted as head above all.

The Psalms are rich in references to God's universal reign. Psalm 22:28 reads: ". . . kingship belongs to the LORD, and he rules over the nations." Listen to Psalm 47:6-7:

---

[2] Herman Ridderbos, *The Coming of the Kingdom*, trans. H. de Jongste, ed. Raymond O. Zorn (Philadelphia, PA: P&R, 1962), 22-23.

> Sing praises to God, sing praises!
> Sing praises to our King, sing praises!
> For God is the King of all the earth;
> Sing praises with a psalm!

Then there is Psalm 99:1-5:

> The LORD reigns; let the peoples tremble!
> He sits enthroned upon the cherubim; let the earth quake!
> The LORD is great in Zion;
> He is exalted over all the peoples.
> Let them praise your great and awesome name!
> Holy is he!
> The King in his might loves justice;
> You have established equity;
> You have executed justice and righteousness in Jacob.
> Exalt the LORD our God;
> Worship at his footstool!
> Holy is he!

In Psalm 103:19 we read: "The LORD has established his throne in the heavens, and his kingdom rules over all," and in Psalm 145:10-13:

> All your works shall give thanks to you, O LORD, and all your saints shall bless you! They shall speak of the glory of your kingdom and tell of your power, to make known to the children of man your mighty deeds, and the glorious splendor of your kingdom. Your kingdom is an everlasting kingdom, and your dominion endures throughout all generations.

In responding to the vision that inaugurated his ministry as prophet, Isaiah exclaimed: "Woe is me! For I am lost; for I am a man of unclean lips, and I dwell in the midst of a people of unclean lips; for my eyes have seen the King; the LORD of hosts!" (Isaiah 6:5). To Israel, Jeremiah pronounced: ". . . the LORD is the true God; he is the living God and the everlasting King. At his wrath the earth quakes, and the nations cannot endure his indignation" (Jeremiah 10:10). Consistently the King is declared to be the LORD of hosts (Jeremiah 46:18; 48:15; 51:57).

In praise of God, King Nebuchadnezzar exclaimed: "How great are his signs, how mighty his wonders! His kingdom is an everlasting kingdom, and his dominion endures from generation to generation" (Daniel 4:3). In a dream he saw the Most High ruling the kingdoms of men (Daniel 4:17). Despite that, Nebuchadnezzar got above himself, proclaiming the glory of his own majesty. As happens, he was brought very low by God until he came to realize that the Most High truly does rule over the kingdoms of men, even over mighty Babylon (Daniel 4:25, 32). Deeply humbled, Nebuchadnezzar came to bless the Most High, praising and honoring him who lives forever:

> For his dominion is an everlasting dominion, and his kingdom endures from generation to generation; all the inhabitants of the earth are accounted as nothing, and he does according to his will among the host of heaven and among the inhabitants of the earth; and none can stay his hand or say to him, "What have you done?" (Daniel 5:34-35; cf., v. 37).

By the time we enter the New Testament, the broad idea of God's universal kingdom is so well established that it is assumed rather than stated. That which was explicit in the Old Testament becomes implicit in the New. Rarely is it referred to overtly. Consider how Peter and John and their friends call on God when faced with the threats of the Sanhedrin. Their prayer begins, "Sovereign Lord, who made the heaven and the earth and the sea and everything in them" (Acts 4:24). Thinking of the mercy he had received in salvation, Paul bursts into one of his spontaneous doxologies: "To the King of ages, immortal, invisible, the only God, be honor and glory forever and ever. Amen" (1 Timothy 1:17). And again, in the same letter, in an obvious rebuttal of Caesar's claim to universal sovereignty, Paul describes God as "the blessed and only Sovereign, the King of kings and Lord of lords, who alone has immortality, who dwells in unapproachable light, whom no one has ever seen or can see. To him be honor and eternal dominion. Amen"

(1 Timothy 6:15-16). This doxology continues in heaven with the song of Moses and of the Lamb:

> Great and amazing are your deeds.
> O Lord God the Almighty!
> Just and true are your ways,
> O King of the nations!
> (Revelation 15:3)

We need say no more. Scripture teaches consistently the unique, eternal, universal reign of God. It is either taught or assumed throughout the Old and New Testaments.

The saving rule of Christ.

In contrast to the universal reign of God, which is referred to explicitly in the Old Testament but assumed in the New, there is another dimension to God's divine rule which is implicit (promised) under the old covenant but explicit (in the process of fulfillment) under the new. I refer to the kingdom of heaven or of God. This we call the mediatorial kingdom of Christ, which God establishes on earth through Christ under the umbrella or within the overall scope of his universal reign. These two notions of kingdom are distinct but inseparable. God rules the entire universe but focuses his universal authority on the progress of Christ's saving reign on earth.

Different authors of the Old Testament underscore that the Creator-God of the universe is specifically the covenant-Lord of his people (e.g., Psalm 68:24-27; 149:2; Isaiah 43:15). According to the Sons of Korah, the reverse is also true: Israel's Lord (formerly referred to in English as Jehovah, now *Yahweh*, and translated "LORD" in Scripture) is none other than the God of the universe— the Lord of hosts! Though transcendent (high above all), his condescending to enter a relationship with his ancient people facilitated their calling him their personal King and their God (Psalm 84:3). They could bank on *Yahweh* for their salvation (Psalm 44:4; 74:12; Isaiah 33:22); their strength, their blessing, and peace

(Psalm 29:10-11). Indeed, so committed has *Yahweh* been in covenant to his people that it is sometimes difficult to discern in certain contexts whether God is referred to as universal King or as the particular King ruling over his people. It seems the two notions can run happily together in an author's mind, for the universal King is also King in a saving sense of God's chosen people (e.g., Psalm 5:2; 10:16).

To underline the arrangement, God, the sovereign Lord of the universe, grants to Israel the standing of a kingdom. In the days of Moses, when Israel was inaugurated at Mount Sinai as a nation, God declared his people to be such (Exodus 19:6). In the kingdom, God would govern by his law. There was the law governing Israel as a body politic, namely, the judicial law. There was also the ceremonial law, educating God's people by means of graphic pictures such as the Tabernacle, the sacrificial system, and the feasts and festivals, of the way he intended to save them from their sins. Moreover, there was the moral law, which mirrored God's righteous and holy character, defined human sin, underlined the need of a Savior, and structured the freedom of all those redeemed by God.

The emphasis falls in the Old Testament not on the kingdom so much as on the King. Although God permitted Israel to have one, he was not to be like the kings of the surrounding nations. In a unique sense Israel's king belonged to *Yahweh*, the Holy One of Israel (Psalm 89:18). For this reason, the ultimate focus of the Israelite was not on the earthly king in Jerusalem but on the divine King in heaven. While *Yahweh* was Israel's true King (Psalm 98:4-6; Jeremiah 8:19), he nevertheless promised to send to his people a coming King.

Recall in 2 Samuel 7:12-16 the wonderful "consolation prize" King David received when his plan to build a temple for the LORD was deferred to his son Solomon:

> When your days are fulfilled and you lie down with your
> fathers, I will raise up your offspring after you, who shall
> come from your body, and I will establish his kingdom. He
> shall build a house for my name, and I will establish the throne
> of his kingdom forever. I will be to him a father, and he shall
> be to me a son. When he commits iniquity, I will discipline
> him with the rod of men, with the stripes of the sons of men,
> but my steadfast love will not depart from him, as I took it
> from Saul, whom I put away before you. And your house and
> your kingdom shall be made sure forever before me. Your
> throne shall be established forever.

This King would be none other than the Son of God whom God
would set on Zion, his holy hill (Psalm 2:6-7). His appearance
would fulfill the LORD's steadfast love to David (Psalm 18:50) as
also the prayer of Solomon, David's son, that God would give the
king justice and the royal son righteousness (Psalm 72:1). What
began as a prayer for himself found ultimate fulfillment in Jesus, the
perfectly just King and faultlessly righteous royal Son (cf., Isaiah
32:1; 33:17).

That fulfillment comes to the fore in the New Testament,
notably in the Gospels where the theme of the kingdom of God is
essential to understanding Christ and his mission.[3] In Jesus the very
kingdom of which Nathan the prophet had spoken to David, drew
near. Christ not only embodied the kingdom of heaven and heralded
the gospel of the kingdom, he authenticated its arrival by displaying
the signs of the kingdom.

Between Jesus' preaching and his performance of these
signs, the message got home that the kingdom of heaven had
arrived. Matthew narrates how, at the climax of his ministry, Jesus
entered triumphantly into Jerusalem in fulfillment of the prophecy of
Zechariah (9:9):

---

[3] Alexander Balmain Bruce, *The Kingdom of God: Christ's Teaching According
to the Synoptic Gospels* (Edinburgh: T&T Clark, 1890), 40.

Say to the daughter of Zion,
"Behold, your king is coming to you,
Humble, and mounted on a donkey,
And on a colt, the foul of a beast of burden."
(Matthew 21:5; cf., Lk. 19:38)

In Mark's account the crowds shouted out, "Hosanna! Blessed is he who comes in the name of the Lord! Blessed is the coming kingdom of our father David! Hosanna in the highest!" (Mark 11:10; cf., Luke 19:38; John 12:15). Whether they knew the coming of the kingdom took more than the advent of Jesus or were admixing in their thinking a spiritual view of Christ's kingdom and political hopes for the overturning of Roman oppression, is uncertain. What is clear is that anyone who had heard Jesus, knew of his claim that in him the kingdom had drawn near. His opponents twisted the claim for their own ends and the blind misunderstood it (e.g., John 19:33-40, and even Acts 1:6), but none could deny that they had heard of it (Luke 23:2).

The securing of the kingdom of heaven required Jesus' death and resurrection. His death broke the power of death and of the devil, and his resurrection ensured his kingdom has a living King with authority to draw to himself all the Father's elect. The fickle crowds on the day of Jesus' triumphal entrance into Jerusalem who, within a week, aided his crucifixion, were superseded in his resurrection and ascension by the authentic worshippers of heaven. David foresaw this a millennium earlier. Listen to them:

Lift up your heads, O gates!
And be lifted up, O ancient doors,
That the King of glory may come in.
Who is this King of glory?
The LORD, strong and mighty,
The LORD, mighty in battle!
(Psalm 24:7-8; repeated in vv. 9-10)

Half a millennium later Daniel also foresaw Christ's victory. In the night he received a vision of the rewarding of Christ for his work:

41

. . . behold, with the clouds of heaven there came one like a son of man, and he came to the Ancient of Days and was presented before him. And to him was given dominion and glory and a kingdom, that all peoples, nations, and languages should serve him; his dominion is an everlasting dominion, which shall not pass away, and his kingdom one that shall not be destroyed. (Daniel 7:13-14).

Christ, then, was guaranteed within the Godhead the spread of the kingdom among all nations in these last days. Whether or not Joseph of Arimathea, a respected member of the Sanhedrin, understood this when asking Pilate for the body of Jesus, we can see with hindsight that he had every reason to "look[ ] for the kingdom of God" (Mark 15:43). Following Christ's exaltation (resurrection and ascension) and his sending of the Spirit at Pentecost, the kingdom spread out from Jerusalem, to Judea, to Samaria, to the uttermost parts of the earth (Acts 1:6-8; 28:30-31). It did so against all opposition from usurpers to Jesus' throne, and has continued to do so (cf., John 19:12-16 and Acts 17:7; Revelation 17:14; 19:16). Jesus had foreseen this during the days of his humiliation. On witnessing the faith of a centurion, he prophesied that "many will come from east and west, and recline at table with Abraham, Isaac, and Jacob in the kingdom of heaven, while the sons of the kingdom will be thrown into the outer darkness. In that place there will be weeping and gnashing of teeth" (Matthew 8:11-12). And again, speaking of the close of the age: ". . . this gospel of the kingdom will be proclaimed throughout the whole world as a testimony to all nations, and then the end will come" (Matthew 24:14).

Only at the Second Advent will the kingdom be fulfilled. Then, writes Paul, Christ will "deliver[ ] the kingdom to God the Father after destroying every rule and every authority and power. For he must reign until he has put all his enemies under his feet" (1 Corinthians 15:24-25; cf., Zechariah 14:9, 16-17). In other words, at his second coming, Christ's mediatorial kingdom, which he has received from the Father to administer by grace for the ingathering of the countless elect, becomes the Father's kingdom.

To this consummated kingdom of elect citizens, the Father gives himself as an inheritance (Matthew 25:34; 26:29 [cf., Luke 22:28-30]). Armed with this knowledge, our lives of fear must give way to those of faith. "Fear not, little flock," said Jesus, "for it is your Father's good pleasure to give you the kingdom" (Luke 12:32). Jesus refers to his people's participation in the divine reign over the redeemed cosmos. We shall not be deified—the Creator-creature distinction is inviolable—but we "will shine like the sun in the kingdom of [our] Father"! (Matthew 13:43).

UNDERSTAND THE PARABLE

Of these two understandings of the kingdom—the universal rule of God and the mediatorial rule of Christ—it is the latter which is so crucial to the parable of the sower. By fleshing out what we mean by Christ's kingdom, we prepare to perceive the strategic significance of Jesus' parables.

The character of Christ's kingdom.

Christ's mediatorial rule is mainly referred to in the New Testament as the kingdom of God (seventy-two times) and the kingdom of heaven (forty-two times). Matthew refers to the theme of the kingdom more than does any other Gospel writer (53 times; cf., Mark, 18 times; Luke, 45 times; and John, 4 times), but he alone refers to Christ's mediatorial reign as the *kingdom of heaven* (although Paul refers to it as the *heavenly kingdom* in 2 Timothy 4:18). On only five occasions does Matthew refer to the kingdom as the *kingdom of God*, for he was writing as a Jew to Jews, mindful of their sensitivities concerning references to *God*. Naturally, Matthew, under the inspiration of the Holy Spirit, makes his own contribution to our understanding of the theme, although his use of *kingdom of heaven* is not so variant that we cannot describe it as normatively interchangeable with the New Testament use of *kingdom of God*.[4]

Regardless of the epithet used, Christ's kingdom is neither a political nor a geographical kingdom. The visibilities of earthly kingdoms—such as borders and constitutions—denote their limitations. The kingdom of heaven by contrast is a spiritual kingdom, sometimes referred to as "a kingdominion." It bespeaks the reign of Christ by his Spirit over the hearts and minds of those who have entered therein. The early twentieth-century poem by diplomat Sir Cecil Spring-Rice (1859–1918), "I vow to thee, my country," while admittedly Christless and patriotic to the point of idolatry in its first verse, nevertheless captures the distinction between the earthly and heavenly kingdom:

> I vow to thee, my country, all earthly things above,
> Entire and whole and perfect, the service of my love:
> The love that asks no question, the love that stands the test,
> That lays upon the altar the dearest and the best;
> The love that never falters, the love that pays the price,
> The love that makes undaunted the final sacrifice.
>
> And there's another country, I've heard of long ago,
> Most dear to them that love her, most great to them that know;
> We may not count her armies, we may not see her King;
> Her fortress is a faithful heart, her pride is suffering;
> And soul by soul and silently her shining bounds increase,
> And her ways are ways of gentleness and all her paths are Peace.

Although the kingdom of heaven is invisible to the human eye, Jesus says that the secrets (literally, the mysteries) of the

---

[4] I am indebted here to Mark Saucy, "The Kingdom-of-God Sayings in Matthew," *Bibliothecra Sacra* 151 (April-June 1994), 176fn.3 (https://faculty.gordon.edu/hu/bi/ted_hildebrandt/ntesources/ntarticles/bsac-nt/saucy-kingdommat-bs.htm, accessed February 14, 2018), and to John F. Walvoord, "The Kingdom of Heaven" (available at https://bible.org/article/kingdom-heaven, also accessed on February 14, 2018).

kingdom have been given to his disciples (Matthew 13:11). When the Pharisees asked Jesus, in Luke 17, when the kingdom of God would come, he answered them: "The kingdom of God is not coming with signs to be observed, nor will they say, 'Look, here it is!' or 'There! For behold, the kingdom of God is in the midst of you" (vv. 20-21). There are those who argue, with good cause, that Luke's record of Jesus should be translated to say that the kingdom is "within you" or "inside of you," for Jesus' point is that the kingdom is invisible to the naked eye. Others prefer the translation "among you" or "in the midst of you" since Jesus would not have said indiscriminately to the Pharisees that the kingdom was represented by them, given their trust in the restoration of theocratic Israel and their hostility toward Jesus. Yet, regardless of the translation, Jesus' point is obvious enough and was understood by the first-century church. Wrote Paul, "the kingdom of God is not a matter of eating and drinking but of righteousness and peace and joy in the Holy Spirit" (Romans 14:17).

Clearly, then, the kingdom of heaven is spiritual. When we talk of entering the kingdom we refer to being one with Christ the King. To belong to the kingdom is to be under his reign. That reign is internal to us. He reigns over our minds, our emotions, and our wills. Christ's kingdom spreads not only within us as he captures more and more of our thinking, feeling, and willing, but from us as, due to his presence, we influence more people to come under his sway.

The spiritual character of the kingdom likely explains why New Testament authors refer to it as the kingdom of God or the kingdom of heaven. Of the latter description, A. B. Bruce writes:

> [The] expression suggests the thought that the kingdom is an ideal hovering over all [better, throughout all] actual societies, civil or sacred. . . . In all probability, the title was used alternatively by Jesus for the express purpose of lifting the minds of the Jewish people into a higher region of thought than

that in which their present hopes as members of the theocratic nation moved.[5]

Typically, the Jews longed for the restoration of the theocracy or kingdom of Israel, but Jesus had something broader and higher, more glorious and mysterious in mind. His people hail him as King, but as a more wonderful King than Israel could ever know, and of a grander and more eternal kingdom than Israel could ever be.

The lessons of Christ's kingdom.

The spirituality of Christ's kingdom is very relevant to the parables. It reminds us, to use the old adage, that a parable is an earthly story with a heavenly meaning. The heavenly meaning has to do with the kingdom of heaven or of God—how we may enter it (and how it enters us) and what expectations there are for those who belong to it. But it also alerts us to several principles.

First, that entrance into the kingdom of heaven cannot be by any visible means, whether by baptism, Christian heritage, nationality, race, or whatever. As we shall see, entrance is by the grace of God alone, operative through the Spirit's gifts of repentance and faith. This means it is possible to be a baptized member of the Christian church, even a communicant member, and yet to remain outside the kingdom (and the kingdom outside of us). What matters ultimately is not our outward connection to the Christian church but our inner connection to Christ. An authentic claim to the latter necessarily involves the former, but the former is no substitute for the latter.

Second, we learn from the spirituality of the kingdom that although the King was born a Jew and first spoke of his kingdom to Jews, its reach surpasses all ethnic and national boundaries. Jesus' teaching of the parable anticipates, then, the spread of the gospel to

---

[5] Bruce, *The Kingdom of God*, 58.

the ends of the earth. It spreads by the power of the Spirit of Christ over one boundary and another, recapturing from the grip of Satan this soul, then that one, and so on. Kings and rulers come and go, but King Jesus continues his unabated and unsurpassed rule of unsullied saving benevolence.

Third, the spirituality of the kingdom reminds us that the primary allegiance of citizens of the kingdom is to Jesus as King. While God would have it, contrary to much demeaning of government in America today, that we should respect the earthly powers he has ordained to rule over us, our allegiance is conditional on their conformity in ruling to his will. The same applies to our respect for leadership in the church and in the home. Our default position is to uphold leadership, but where authorities in family, church, or state conflict with the will of God revealed in his Word, then it is to Christ, speaking through his Word, that we are to submit. Neither king, nor court of state or church, nor parent at home has the right to subvert or to suppress the will of Christ. He is Lord of the conscience. When he commands, we are to obey, beginning with the call to turn to God in repentance and to rest on Christ in faith. It is to our advantage that we heed him.

The parable of the sower is one of Jesus' prominent test cases as to whether we have heeded him. Christ calls us through the parable to submit to him as King. Only those doing so can authentically claim Jesus as theirs. Only those who can, may claim to be citizens of his kingdom, favored and protected by Christ as King. In short, there is no belonging to the kingdom without repentance unto God and faith in Christ's person and work.

The teaching of Christ's kingdom.

The Jews were very familiar with parables. Although a *mashal* could refer to multiple rhetorical forms such as fable and apothegm (an instructive saying or maxim), in so far as it bespeaks a parable, a *mashal* "signif[ies] an artificial narrative of a thing done, to signify another thing."[6] It is said that there are as few as five of these in the Old Testament (2 Samuel 12:1-4; 14:6-8; 1 Kings 20:39-40; Isaiah 5:1-6; Isaiah 28:24-28), but the Jews made the genre theirs during the four-hundred-year intertestamental period prior to the coming of Christ.

Jesus' parables were not, then, unique. They, writes Peter Williams, "frequently contain traditional Jewish themes rearranged to make his own, often surprising, conclusions." His parables of the sower, the good Samaritan, and the prodigal son are, Williams continues, recognized as "masterpieces of composition," revealing Jesus to be, apart from so much else, the creative genius behind the founding of Christianity.[7] More than that, Jesus' parables proclaim his eternal kingdom as the immediate focus of Christianity. "Nothing distinctly approaching its [Jesus' parabolic form of teaching] depth and power, its felicitous brevity and manifold applications," writes Frederic Farrar, "can be produced either from the Old Testament, or from the entire literature of humanity either before or since His life on earth."[8] In other words, Jesus' parables are weightier than any others known to man.

So profound was Jesus' teaching of the kingdom that it is given us not only in the parable of the sower but also in its interpretation. In fact, the parable of the sower is but one of only two recorded which Jesus interprets. The other is the parable of the weeds which follows immediately in Matthew's narrative (13:24-30, 36-43). It seems significant that interpretations only accompany the

---

[6] Benjamin Keach draws from German theologian Salomo Glassius (1593–1656) in *Exposition of the Parables*, 2. I am also indebted in this paragraph to the *Jewish Encyclopedia: The unedited full-text of the 1906 Jewish Encyclopedia* (www.jewishencyclopedia.com/articles/10459-mashal, accessed January 21, 2019).
[7] Peter J. Williams, *Can We Trust the Gospels?* (Wheaton, IL: Crossway, 2018), 102-103.
[8] Frederic W. Farrar, *The Life of Christ*, "The Quiver" Edition (London, *et al.*: Cassell, 1896), 227-228.

first two. It is as if Jesus teaches his disciples (or Matthew informs his readers) how to read them, saying in effect, "Here are a few sample interpretations of Jesus to get you going in interpreting the parables for yourselves." "They exhibit," says Alfred Edersheim, "the elementary truths concerning the planting of the Kingdom of God, its development, reality, value, and final vindication."[9]

Interestingly, the connection between the kingdom of heaven and the parable of the sower comports with the original meaning of the term *parabolē*: to rule or to govern. Benjamin Keach gleans from it several ideas which he attributes to Joseph Caryl (1602–1673). As sentences of wisdom or truth, parables:

- Rule over the spirits of men by the convincing light they shed.
- Come from the mouths of princes and great persons.
- Are the yardstick by which our judgments, actions, and opinions are tried, for they are touchstones of truth or rules, whether a person submits to them or not.[10]

Now whereas basic similes are identifiable by the use of "like" or "as" and simply state that "A" is like "B", parables are larger pictorial similitudes communicating a greater amount of truth since the whole picture conveyed by the parable is relevant.[11] Specifically, parables:

- Pictorialize familiar details in life so as to impress upon the memory what a given parable teaches.
- Stimulate the study of their meaning.
- Search the conscience and arouse emotion.

---

[9] Alfred Edersheim, *The Life and Times of Jesus the Messiah*, Volume 1 (New York: Longmans, Green, and Co., 1910), 579.

[10] Keach, *Exposition of the Parables*, xiv.

[11] Similes are to parables what metaphors are to models (robust metaphors), and *vice versa*.

- Offer insight into the deep things of God (the mysteries of the kingdom).[12]

That said, we are not to read the parables with what Alfred Edersheim calls "strict scientific accuracy."[13]

Jesus intended the parables to serve as practical illustrations of truth. It was not his purpose for us to get so absorbed by the picture he paints that we miss the principles he was in earnest to teach. He thus offered not a fault-proof depiction of the earthly scenes envisioned, but one sufficiently realistic to unveil the mysteries of the kingdom. As such, Jesus' parables are accommodated to our limited human capacities—capacities which are finite enough to require parables to understand the kingdom, but not so finite that we cannot appreciate their illustrative qualities. To claim, then, that Jesus misunderstood the scenarios from which he drew the parables is to miss their purpose and function. Jesus thought up parables to illustrate the kingdom, and not the kingdom to illustrate the parables. Any deviation from the actuality of the familiar scenes he paints serves to ensure an accurate picture of his kingdom.

This all goes to say that while the parable is an earthly story with a heavenly meaning, there is an urgency to it that the definition fails to capture. The parable attests whether we are Christ's and destined for an eternity with him, or are outside of his kingdom, in the grip of the devil, and bound for an eternity without Christ. The parable of the sower may speak of four soils but there are only two conditions depicted. Either we are Christ's and growing in submission to him, or we are not. In which case, we are rebelling against him, a fact which no amount of christianese (cultural "Christianity') can eradicate or overcome.

---

[12] Keach, *Exposition of the Parables*, 3.
[13] Alfred Edersheim, *The Life and Times of Jesus the Messiah*, 592.

STUDY QUESTIONS: SESSION TWO

1. Describe in your own words what the Bible means by the kingdom.

2. Discuss specific differences between the kingdom of heaven and the kingdoms of men.

3. How do we enter the kingdom of heaven? How does this entrance highlight differences between Christ's kingdom and his church?

4. What does it mean to belong to the kingdom of heaven or for the kingdom of heaven to enter us?

5. How ought the reach of the kingdom to impact our attitudes concerning ethnic diversities?

6. How does the kingship of Christ impact our allegiance to parents, employers, civil authority?

7. Why is the kingdom of heaven so significant for understanding the parable of the sower?

Prayer: Sovereign Lord, enlighten our minds, touch our hearts, and direct our wills as we seek to understand your kingly rule. We praise you for your particular interest in your people and for your establishment through Christ of the kingdom of heaven. Show us, we humbly pray, where we stand in relation to it, and guide our thoughts as we come to this parable of the kingdom. In Jesus' name we pray. Amen.

In preparation for chapter three, read: Matthew 4:18-25; 8:1–12:50; 13:1-2, 10-17.

3.

THE PARABLE AND THE CROWD

[1] That same day Jesus went out of the house and sat beside the sea. [2] And great crowds gathered about him, so that he got into a boat and sat down. And the whole crowd stood on the beach.

Matthew 13:1-2

[10] Then the disciples came and said to him, "Why do you speak to them in parables?" [11] And he answered them, "To you it has been given to know the secrets of the kingdom of heaven, but to them it has not been given. [12] For to the one who has, more will be given, and he will have an abundance, but from the one who has not, even what he has will be taken away. [13] This is why I speak to them in parables, because seeing they do not see, and hearing they do not hear, nor do they understand. [14] Indeed, in their case the prophecy of Isaiah is fulfilled that says:

"'You will indeed hear but never understand, and you will indeed see but never perceive. [15] For this people's heart has grown dull, and with their ears they can barely hear, and their eyes they have closed, lest they should see with their eyes and hear with their ears and understand with their heart and turn, and I would heal them.'

Matthew 13:10-15

Having alluded to the vital connection between the kingdom of heaven and the parable of the sower, we now zoom in a little further to consider that between the parable and the crowd who first heard it. In doing so, we enter Matthew's Gospel. There we find a notable triangulation of the ideas: the kingdom, the parable, and the crowd. The kingdom of heaven supplies the structure of the Gospel, the parable Jesus' means of preaching the kingdom, and the crowd the need of doing so.

Frederic Farrar observes that in Matthew's Gospel (and Mark's) the content is organized around the author's subjective considerations and is, therefore, arranged according to its spiritual or moral bearings.[1] Which is to say that Matthew gears his account of Christ's life to the need of his predominantly Jewish readers to understand that Jesus is the long-promised King. Note how this plays out:

- In 1:1–4:16 Matthew focuses on *the identity of the king*. Recall his recording of the inquiry of the magi upon their arrival in Jerusalem: "Where is he who has been born king of the Jews?" (2:2).

- Then, from 4:17–16:21 Matthew narrates *the discourses and actions of the king*, beginning with, "Repent, for the kingdom of heaven is at hand."

- Finally, from 16:20–28:22 he depicts his *sufferings and conquest of the king*.

These divisions are not arbitrary or artificially constructed by Matthew, nor are they imposed on Matthew's Gospel by New Testament scholars or by preachers looking for a neat arrangement of their treatments of the Gospel. Rather, the structure arises from within Matthew's account of the life and ministry of Jesus. Note the exact wording with which 4:17 and 16:21 begin:

---

[1] Luke, by contrast, "pays more attention to the natural sequence, although he also occasionally allows a unity of subject to supersede in his arrangement the order of time" (Frederic W. Farrar, *The Life of Christ*, "The Quiver" Edition (London, *et al.*: Cassell, 1896), 227.

> From that time [*Apò tóte*] Jesus began to preach, saying, "Repent, for the kingdom of heaven is at hand." (4:17)
>
> From that time [*Apò tóte*] Jesus began to show his disciples that he must go to Jerusalem and suffer many things from the elders and chief priests and scribes, and be killed, and on the third day be raised. (16:20)

Clearly, Matthew uses the refrain "From that time" as a section marker to identify his transition from one section of the Gospel and one aspect of the kingdom to the next. First, from his compilation of the narrative around the identity of the King to his discourses, and then from his discourses to his sufferings and conquest.

The parable of the sower is found in the middle section of the Gospel, where Matthew records Jesus' discourses or lessons about the kingdom. Chapter thirteen is particularly relevant, for this is where he begins to speak of the kingdom of heaven in parables, commencing with the parable of the sower. He issues the parable, it follows, with royal authority, commanding us to hear it. His expectation of our obedience arises not from an inferiority complex, as if, like an insecure leader rising as in the Peter Principle to a prominence beyond his skill-set or experience, he gives the directive merely because he can.[2] Rather, Jesus commands those crowding about him to hear the parable out of love for his hearers and out of concern for his Father's honor. He commands us by extension, to listen to his parable and to what it says of the kingdom of heaven.

By the time we catch up with him in Matthew 13, his ministry has been under way for some time. This begs the question as to why Jesus, only then, began to speak in parables. The answer lies in the turning point to which his ministry had arrived.

---

[2] The Peter Principle comes from a book published in 1968 under that title by Canadian Laurence J. Peter. In it he observed that employees in organizations tend to rise through promotions to a level at which they finally prove to be incompetent.

THE TURNING POINT TRACED

As we noted in the previous chapter, Jesus' proclamation that the kingdom had arrived (4:17) was quickly and clearly authenticated by many remarkable signs. States Matthew, Jesus

> went throughout Galilee teaching in their synagogues and proclaiming the gospel of the kingdom and healing every disease and every affliction among the people. So his fame spread throughout all Syria, and they brought him all the sick, those afflicted with various diseases and pains, those oppressed by demons and epileptics, and paralytics, and he healed them, And great crowds followed him from Galilee and the Decapolis, and from Jerusalem and Judea, and from beyond the Jordan. (4:23-25; cf., 9:35)

The signs confirmed the "gospel of the kingdom" Jesus preached (cf., 9:35). A leper was cleansed (8:1-4), Peter's mother-in-law was raised up (8:14-15), many oppressed with demons were freed (8:16, 28-34; 12:27), and countless other sick were healed in fulfillment of Old Testament prophecy (8:16-17; 9:1-8, 20-22; 11:15). What is more, Jesus calmed a storm (8:23-27), raised a girl to life (9:18-26), and healed the blind and the mute (9:27-34). This was just the start. The healing of the centurion's servant portended the gospel of the kingdom going out to the Gentiles (8:5-13), as did the appointment of the twelve apostles (9:35–10:15).

In contrast to much preaching nowadays, Jesus taught not only how to enter the kingdom but what is expected of those who do so. He came not only to save sinners but to rule over them for his Father's glory and for their good. In calling his first disciples (who were to be his apostles [cf., 4:18-22; 9:9-13; and 10:1-4]) Jesus reminds us that those entering the kingdom are no longer their own. We are from henceforth to serve divine purposes. Yet, far from advertising the kingdom like a secondhand car as "sold as seen," hoping the buyer will not be put off by any downsides, Jesus openly talked of those values of kingdom-life flowing against the stream of the world's preferences (see, for example, the Sermon on the Mount [Matthew 5–7]). These values not only set citizens of his kingdom apart from society, they often place them at odds with the cultural values of their day. Thus, while Jesus calls his hearers to ask, to seek, and to knock for entrance into the kingdom, they must count the cost of entering the kingdom before doing so (8:18-22). After all, there would come a time when he would no longer be present with them in the flesh. They would mourn his absence and fast for his return (9:14-15), for persecution was coming their way. The persecution would begin with the apostles (10:16-25) and was anticipated by the beheading of John the Baptist (11:1-19). Jesus, though, brought his own kind of sword, not to fight hatred with hatred, but through spiritual battle to pry his people from the evil one (10:26-42).

Such an evenhanded depiction of the blessings and burdens of belonging to the kingdom of heaven would inevitably sift Jesus' hearers. Some came by God's grace to understand the spiritual significance of the kingdom. These heeded his warning concerning the unrepentant of Chorazin and Bethsaida (11:20-24) and opted to take up Jesus' loving command to come to him for rest. In doing so, they trusted his gentleness and lowliness of heart for their forgiveness and acceptance (11:25-30). Although the full picture of his identity was hidden from their sight, they knew enough to submit to his reign over their lives, thankful that for all his great power he neither breaks the bruised reed nor snuffs out the smoldering wick (12:15-21).

Others, however, saw the kingdom of heaven as a threat to their personal domains. Of no one was this more so than the Pharisees who claimed that Jesus was Beelzebub, the prince of demons (12:23-30). There was no shortage of people to believe them. Jesus responded that those demeaning him could be forgiven but warned that any resisting the Holy Spirit would remain unforgiven, both in this age and in the age to come (12:32). While the Spirit points and draws people to Jesus, it does not follow that he is any less than Jesus in the Godhead or that Jesus takes it lightly when the Spirit's ministry is resisted. To resist his ministry is not only to grieve God, it is to remain adrift from Christ and his kingdom. Only by the Spirit are we able to repent toward God and to rest in faith upon the Lord Jesus (12:22-32). The scribes and Pharisees didn't get the memo. By continuing to harass Jesus they confirmed their eternal plight. "Teacher, we wish to see a sign from you" (12:38). The request was, of course, disingenuous, for Jesus had worked signs of the kingdom among them all along! So many of them in fact that he had gathered about him the very crowds the scribes and Pharisees so envied. Such signs are now historical, but they shall yet testify against the scribes and Pharisees at the end of the age.

Amid the standoff stood the crowds of ordinary folk. Who would they follow? Christ or his implacable enemies? Certainly, they were interested in Christ, fascinated even, but would this intrigue result over time in their becoming his committed disciples? The crowds must bring forth good fruit if they were to be counted as authentic followers of Jesus (12:33-36). The same goes for those freed from demon possession. They must be in the kingdom and under the reign of Christ if they are to avoid being overrun by seven spirits (12:43-45). It follows then, in chapter thirteen, that belonging to the crowd surrounding Jesus is not the same as belonging to his kingdom. Time tells us again and again that no matter how interested we may be in Christ at any given point in our lives, unless we have entered his kingdom and have submitted to his reign we shall eventually reveal ourselves to be against him. The revelation may be subtle or out there, but the truth remains: If we are not for Jesus, we are against him.[3]

---

[3] This claim may, on a superficial reading, appears to contradict Jesus' words in Luke 9:50. There he responds to John's concern about someone casting out

Jesus knew this very well. In the verses immediately preceding the parable of the sower we read of him, earlier in the day, underlining what was most important to him. While addressing the people, a man approached him informing him that his mother and brothers were asking to speak with him. "Who is my mother, and who are my brothers?" Jesus responded. Gesticulating toward his disciples, he declared, "Here are my mother and my brothers! For whoever does the will of my Father in heaven is my brother and sister and mother" (12:46-50). Jesus thereby laid down the principle so needed by each of us in our day that sincere obedience to Christ counts more to him than do the numbers hanging around him.

Thus, in Matthew chapter thirteen, Jesus begins to give weighty expression to his burden for the souls in the crowd. How many of those thronging him were prepared to submit to him for forgiveness and his gracious instilling of order and purpose in their lives? To answer that question, Jesus began to distinguish more proactively his apostles and disciples from the crowd. His nuancing of the spiritual standing of the masses before him was not for his information but for their spiritual welfare. The limitation of their interest in Jesus to his satisfaction of their temporal needs gave the game away. Jesus' signs of the kingdom had become in the eyes of the crowd ends in themselves. Many were blinded by self-interest to the purpose of the miracles as specific *signs of the kingdom.* This did not make Jesus indifferent to the needs of the crowds. He cared deeply about them, but he stopped short of empowering their consumerism. He insisted that their spiritual needs were greatest of all. Instead, then, of giving them only what they wanted, as we would a spoiled child or puppy, Jesus set about keeping central his message of the kingdom.

---

demons in Jesus' name, stating, "Do not stop him, for the one who is not against you is for you." However, there Jesus was speaking of the ministry of his people, whereas here I am speaking of those yet to become such.

This determination began "that same day" (13:1). From the fact that his mother and brothers had "stood outside" (12:46), we surmise that Jesus had been in the house in Capernaum. He now leaves it to sit beside the Sea of Galilee. Obviously, the crowds could not all fit in the house, but they could gather about him along the shore. So much so, that Jesus retreated into a moored boat. There he sat to teach the crowds.

This was a posture adopted by rabbis before their devotees. They would teach from place to place, sometimes in the marketplace, and sometimes under the shade of a tree. Jesus' teaching from a boat fits, then, the picture of a rabbi of the period. By sitting to teach he signifies his authority to do so. Like most rabbis of his day, he came from Galilee, and mirrored the characteristics of a rabbi's ministry: a preoccupation with the theme of the kingdom of God, a choice of disciples to follow him, and a couching of his teaching in parables. Yet, there was something different about his rabbinical teaching. When he taught the kingdom of heaven he did so *as the King*! In opening his mouth to teach he did so with a *royal* authority. It is no wonder that his fame as rabbi would far outlast that of the most renowned rabbis of the first and second centuries *anno Domini*: Johanan ben Zakkai; his pupil, Hanina ben Dosa; Abba Yose Holikufri, Zadok, Halaphta, and Hananian ben Teradyon.

Yet, neither fame nor men-pleasing motivated Jesus. So long as the crowds remained more taken by his signs than by his kingdom, they would receive nothing eternal from him. The kingdom you see, is only for those surrendering to him. The same goes for the uncommitted flooding today's churches to hear more of their felt needs than of God's glory. Preach repentance toward God and faith in Jesus Christ, submission to his reign in the details of life, and a dying to self in the cause of glorifying God, and how many of the crowds will leg it for the next self-serving fad. Their best life now as they perceive it is not their best life as God envisions it, nor can it extend to the next life. The life to come, Scripture teaches us, is gain only to those spending this life in grateful response to God's grace in Christ (cf., Philippians 1:21).

THE TURNING POINT EXPLAINED

Faced with the mixed motives of the crowd, Jesus began to preach in parables. Whether he thought of the parables prior to using them, or in the moment as he sat in the boat facing the shore—either is feasible—we do not know. Clearly, they have stood the test of time and continue to speak to us today amid the christianese of our culture.

The first series of parables, numbering seven in Matthew 13, responds to the particular unreceptiveness of the crowds. Jesus' later series in Luke 10–16 and 18 speaks more to the opposition of the Pharisees. Whereas the crowds were marked by passive indifference, the Pharisees were actively hostile.[4] It is in regard to the latter series that Jesus' parables have been defined as "hand grenades lobbed into enemy territory." By contrast, the first series of parables **is** pointed but less confrontational. It enabled Jesus to minister on his own terms to those willing to hear him, while simultaneously inaugurating a preliminary judgment on those who witnessed his signs of the kingdom and who heard his invitation to enter it, but who willfully remained unrepentant and held back from trusting him. Jesus thus began making use of familiar scenes from everyday life, whether real or imagined, to encourage his true disciples and to chide those neglecting their opportunities to enter the kingdom.

In the sequence of Matthew's narrative, Jesus first told the parable (vv. 3-9), then, upon request, he explained to his disciples why he began speaking in parables (vv. 10-17). Finally, he supplied the interpretation (vv. 18-23). We shall come to the parable and its

---

[4] Alfred Edersheim, *The Life and Times of Jesus the Messiah*, Volume 1 (New York: Longmans, Green, and Co., 1910), 579-580.

interpretation (vv. 3-9 and 18-23) in part two. Here we consider Jesus' response to his disciples' question, "Why do you speak to them [the crowds] in parables?" (v. 10). The answer Matthew records has three elements.

The observation (vv. 11-13).

First, Jesus distinguishes those receiving God's grace (the disciples) from those ignoring it (the crowds). Whereas the disciples have "been given to know the secrets (literally, the mysteries) of the kingdom," the crowds are left in their spiritual indifference.

French Protestant theologian Edouard Reuss (1804–1891) describes a mystery (in the biblical sense) as "a truth revealed for the first time by Jesus only, and by the Spirit of God who continues His work, and unknown to previous generations."[5] The disciples could not, then, have come by the knowledge of the kingdom naturally—that is to say, by means of intelligence, learning, or intuition. The mysteries were revealed and understood by divine illumination alone. While their revelation was packaged in parables given at specific points in time, the illumination of the minds of the disciples occurred over time, hence their initial need of an explanation.

By contrast, Jesus warns the crowds of the danger of coming face-to-face with him only to reject his spiritual and eternal reign in favor of their own earthly and temporal "kingdoms." Whereas every last one of their kingdoms would fail, his does not. So, rather than stand back in self-congratulation, admiring the many he has gathered about him, Jesus compartmentalizes the people before him into two sorts: those possessing the secret of the kingdom (his

---

[5] Quoted by A. B. Bruce, *The Kingdom of God: Christ's Teaching According to the Synoptic Gospels* (Edinburgh: T&T Clark, 1890), 49.

apostles and disciples) and those blind to it (the crowds). He is, to quote Herman Ridderbos, "draw[ing] a line through His listeners."[6]

Jesus does not explain how God sovereignly withholds from the crowds the mysteries of the kingdom and yet holds them responsible for not getting beyond their material concerns. Yet, clearly, he states that they *are* responsible. In their fallenness, they had not considered the costs of belonging to the kingdom worthwhile. They were, therefore, left in their dire spiritual condition. His parables are, in this light, a proverbial way of saying, in the words of his Sermon on the Mount, that he would no longer give the dogs what is holy or cast his pearls before swine (Matthew 7:6). Jesus sought not to offend, certainly not in a sinful way, but he was bent on upholding the preciousness of the gospel he had proclaimed and the responsibility which accompanies the privilege of hearing it preached.

To quote nineteenth-century churchman J. C. Ryle: "Men are apt to forget that it does not require great open sins to be sinned in order to ruin a soul forever."[7] All it takes is the quietest refusal to come under the reign of Christ. God, we ought to recall, reads our minds, knows our hearts, and observes our wills. Once our rejection of Christ wafts up to heaven, we are in the precarious position of provoking God's righteous displeasure. Although he is slow to anger, it is within his prerogative to take from us the opportunities given to respond to Christ. The crowds of Jesus' day would come to picture his face in their memories, as also the words of his teaching and the power of his miracles, but without repentance and faith in Christ, their fading recollections would be all that remained to them of the opportunity on earth to enter the kingdom. These memories

---

[6] H. N. Ridderbos, *Matthew*, Bible Student's Commentary, trans. Ray Togtman (Grand Rapids: Regency Reference Library [Zondervan], 1987), 254.
[7] J. C. Ryle, *Expository Thoughts on Matthew*, first published 1856 (Carlisle, PA: The Banner of Truth Trust, 1986), 96.

will yet return to haunt them at the end of the age when they stand before King Jesus. Meanwhile, the divergent responses to Jesus opened up a yawning spiritual chasm between the crowds and the disciples. In time, the former would go their way as would also those disciples proving to be false professors. Christ's authentic disciples, however, would become increasingly separated unto God.

The pronouncement (vv. 14-16).

Second, Jesus declares that the situation unfolding before him was a fulfilment of the prophecy of Isaiah (Isaiah 6:9-10). Isaiah was called to the office of prophet during a time in which God's people were refusing the divine call to repent. The Lord commissioned Isaiah to go and say to his people that they would keep on hearing from him, but would not understand, and would keep on seeing but not perceive. Yet, the more they resisted Isaiah's prophetic call to turn back to God, the more they became dull of heart—meaning that their ears became heavy and their eyes blind. They were, accordingly, the means of their own spiritual hardening. While self-inflicted, the hardening was, and remains, God's judgment on impenitence.

Defying modern notions of a "successful ministry," God called Isaiah to keep on preaching to Judah until his judgment on her was complete. Understandably, Isaiah inquired of God how long he was to preach such a message to the people. Back came the answer:

> "Until cities lie waste without inhabitant,
> And houses without people,
> And the land is a desolate waste,
> And the LORD removes people far away,
> And the forsaken places are many in the midst of the land.
> And though a tenth remain in it,
> It will be burned again,
> Like a terebinth or an oak,
> Whose stump remains when it is felled."
> (Isaiah 6:11-13)

According to Jesus, the ultimate fulfillment of this judgment occurred not in Isaiah's day or through the prophet's ministry, but in his own day and through his own ministry.

Speaking of the crowds before him, Jesus pronounced to his disciples, "the prophecy of Isaiah is fulfilled" (v. 14). He quotes it from the Septuagint (the Greek translation of the Hebrew Scriptures), inserting one important adjustment. Whereas in Isaiah 6 the sovereign Lord (*Adonay*) calls Isaiah to make the hearts of the people dull lest *they* should turn and be healed, in Matthew 13 Jesus adapts the prophecy to read "lest . . . I would heal them" (Isaiah 6:8, 10; Matthew 13:15). He reveals thereby not only his oneness with *Adonay*, the sovereign Lord, but also the double-sided effectiveness of his ministry, granting understanding to those turning penitently to God and judgment on those refusing to. (v. 15).

In his use of Isaiah's prophecy, Jesus implicitly indicts his hearers' intellectual pride. Although a down-to-earth people, the crowds were sitting as God's ancient people on a treasure trove of divine revelation. They heard it read in the synagogue each Sabbath. It pointed to the Messiah. Nevertheless, for all the signs Jesus gave of his Messiahship and of his fulfillment of the promise of an eternal king, the crowds refused to recognize Jesus as such. Quite the opposite! The more they heard him preach, the less they listened to what he told them of the kingdom, and the more miracles they witnessed the less they perceived in them its arrival.

This is not solely a Jewish problem. Centuries later, Paul, an apostle to the Gentiles, lamented in a letter to the Corinthians about how the gospel was veiled to the perishing: ". . . the god of this world has blinded the minds of the unbelievers, to keep from seeing the light of the gospel of the glory of Christ, who is the image of God" (2 Corinthians 4:3-4). So it is today, especially among those who have had every privilege of hearing the gospel but have preferred either Christian stuff, the world, or both to Christ. If you recognize yourself in this, and are concerned to do so, you are not yet blinded. Therefore, heed Christ now by coming to God through him, while you may.

The benediction (vv. 16-17).

Third, in contrast to his indictment of the crowds, Jesus encourages his disciples: ". . . blessed are *your* eyes, for they see, and *your* ears, for they hear" (italics inserted). It is as if Jesus pointed at his disciples, singling them out, to assure them emphatically, "Yes, *you* are blessed! *Your* eyes see, and *your* ears hear!" Indeed, the Greek confirms this emphasis.

This is a wonderful truth everyone belonging to Christ's kingdom can claim, but there was a particular poignancy in Jesus' assuring of his disciples that day: ". . . truly, I say to you, many prophets and righteous people longed to see, and did not see it, and to hear what you hear, and did not hear it" (v. 17). This does not mean to say that the Old Testament prophets saw nothing of Jesus. Jesus proclaimed to the Jews that their Father Abraham had rejoiced to see his day and was glad (John 8:56). What is more, they could see him in faith through the Old Testament sacrificial system and, to a degree, in Theophanies (the appearance of God to human senses).[8] The prophets "forthtold" God's Word to the people and foretold of the coming Messiah. They witnessed the failures of the kings who ruled over them, and doubtless yearned for one to rule in righteousness and in kindness (Psalm 72:1-4ff.). Yet neither the prophets nor the righteous saw the Messiah incarnate. They could

---

[8] There is some merit to the argument that, as regards the Old Testament, the term Theophany (the manifestation of God) is more appropriate than the term Christophany (the manifestation of Christ), since the Trinity, although implied in Old Testament times, had not yet been revealed. On this understanding, Christophany is a term restricted to the New Testament's post-ascension appearances of Jesus.

not look him in the eyes, hear his audible voice, or observe his ministry's other-worldly phenomena.

How privileged were those, by contrast, who truly heard Jesus that day! The apostle Peter was one of them. Later, he passed along our Lord's encouragement to his readers scattered throughout Pontus, Galatia, Cappadocia, Asia, and Bithynia:

> Concerning this salvation, the prophets who prophesied about the grace that was to be yours searched and inquired carefully, inquiring what person or time the Spirit of Christ in them was indicating when he predicted the sufferings of Christ and the subsequent glories. It was revealed to them that they were serving not themselves but you, in the things that have now been announced to you through those who preached the good news to you by the Holy Spirit sent from heaven, things into which angels long to look. (1 Peter 1:10-12).

Amazing! The holiest and most anointed individuals of the old covenant era could not see what the lowly disciples—a seemingly random band of ex-fisherman, a marginalized tax-collector, and the like—could see as they listened in to Jesus, the one long promised. Although the disciples were, like the rest of humankind, made "a little lower than the heavenly beings" (Psalm 8:5), their recreation raised them higher than the angelic order. Grace, you see, elevates us to a plane of understanding beyond the reach of the heavenly beings. Although they inhabit heaven and we earth, God enables us to see, to hear, and to understand his saving grace in Christ in ways in which the angels cannot. Even if they could, the fallen angels do not receive God's grace and the unfallen angels do not need it. By contrast, we who rest on Christ not only receive God's forgiveness, we gain insight into the extent of his condescension and mercy in the Savior.

To confirm this, Matthew comments later in chapter thirteen that Jesus now "said nothing to [the crowd and the disciples] without a parable" (v. 34). What was being hidden from the crowds was being revealed to the disciples in fulfillment of Old Testament Scripture, the Psalm of Asaph (78:2):

> "I will open my mouth in parables;
> I will utter what has been hidden
> Since the foundation of the world."

In the meantime, Jesus forewarned his disciples that if the crowds continued to reject him, even what they had received from him would be taken from them (v. 12). They would lose not only the opportunity to learn of the kingdom of heaven, but whatever sort of desire they had to do so. The unfallen angels continue yearning to look into salvation, but not the crowds whose judgment was inaugurated in preliminary fashion by their refusal to listen to Jesus.

THE TURNING POINT APPLIED

Jesus opens both the parable and its interpretation by reminding us that as amazing a privilege as it is to hear from God, we nevertheless need to be directed to do so. Notice the repeated commands included in the synoptic accounts of Jesus' parable.

The command to all to hear the parable.

Mark's account of the parable begins as follows:

Again he began to teach beside the sea. And a very large crowd gathered about him, so that he got into a boat and sat in it on the sea, and the whole crowd was beside the sea on the land. And he was teaching them many things in parables, and in his teaching he said to them: "Listen!" (Mark 4:1-3a).

The command—ἀκούετε, a second person plural present imperative active, meaning to go on listening—is the first word of the parable in Mark's account. No matter who we are and whether we follow him or not, Jesus says to us in effect that it his will that we note the lessons of the parable. We are not only to listen to him but to keep on listening.

As universal as is this command, in what follows we especially focus on the need of those yet outside the kingdom to hear the parable. They fell, and fall, into different categories.

First, there were those who, at the time of Jesus' teaching of the parable could not possibly have heard the parable. We might be forgiven for assuming that those of the nations were alleviated of the obligation to hear it. Certainly, they were free of culpability at the time. They did not have the privileges Israel had. The apostle Paul later listed these as Israel's adoption as God's Son, his sighting of the glory of God, his participation in the covenants God initiated with his people, his receipt of the divinely given law, the privilege of worship according to God's revealed regulations, and the assurance of God's gracious promises (Romans 9:4). Nor did they have the presence of Christ among them and ready access to his teaching, hence God's historic forbearance with their sins (Acts 17:30; Romans 3:25).

Nevertheless, the surrounding peoples were not without indications of God's existence and his desire to relate to our human race. Indeed, by the time of Jesus' parable, God's forbearance had nearly run its course. The moves he had made to encourage the nations to seek him were reaching a climax in the sending of Christ and, in the near future, the sending of the Spirit:

- *God had revealed himself in nature to all humankind.* From creation God has been declaring his glory to the human race, manifesting his invisible attributes to us, all day, all night, in the hearing and understanding of all, and in all places (cf., Psalm 19:1-4 and Romans 1:18-20).

- *God had created man in his image.* As the crown of creation, man received a special privilege and role as God's image bearer. To this end, God etched ineradicably on the

69

constitution of man the knowledge of himself, irrespective of his place in history or in the world.

- *God had granted the nations some light.* Although God revealed himself particularly solely to Israel, he called his chosen people to be a light dispelling the darkness of the nations. Those who looked to God's people got some sense of God and of his saving purposes. The Canaanites of Jericho knew it was the Lord God who had brought the children of Israel out of Egypt through the Red Sea, the desert, and the battles against the Amorite kings, Sihon and Og (Joshua 2:8-11). Nebuchadnezzar knew it was the Lord God of heaven who revealed the mysteries of his dreams to Daniel (Daniel 2:46-48; cf., 4:9). He knew of the true God not only from the knowledge of him inscribed on his constitution, but because God's people, for all their sins, took with them into exile their hope in the coming Messiah. Doubtless, this messianic hope also influenced the magi five centuries later when they came to search for the king of the Jews (Matthew 2:1-12).

- *God had now given to the world his Son.* Despite the exiles of the northern and southern kingdoms of Israel and Judah, the global influence of God's people was limited. Israel could only shed the light of the gospel so far. Moreover, the frequent disobedience and faithlessness of God's covenant people dimmed the gospel light that Israel could dispel, hence God's prior forbearance with the nations. That said, it was from the Jews that the Messiah came. Having completed the work his Father gave him to do and having been raised from death as a proof of the fact, Jesus gave marching orders to his people, commanding them as from his sending of the Spirit at Pentecost to take the gospel from Jerusalem to the ends of the earth.

Such encouragements were, of themselves, insufficient to save the nations, but they were enough to stir them to search for God, for a relationship with him. The arrival of the magi in Jerusalem in search of the king of the Jews and the faith of the centurion are examples from Matthew's Gospel alone demonstrating the culpability of the nations for not seeking God (Matthew 2:1-12; 8:5-13).

Second, there were those more culpable since they experienced Jesus firsthand and had the living Word in their sights and in their hearing. I refer to the crowds before Jesus who had grown up amid the history and practice of Judaism. Each man would have been given in infancy the sign and seal of the covenant, namely, circumcision. They partook of the feasts of the Hebrew calendar and brought their sacrifices to the temple, as their ancestors had to the tabernacle complex before them. Yet, it had always been the case in Israel that there were those circumcised in the flesh but not in the heart. They were part of the visible community of God's people but were without a personal relationship to God. Thinking back on the history of God's ancient people, Paul later remarked that, "not all who are descended from Israel belong to Israel" (Romans 9:6). All Israel had exposure to the privileges of God's ancient people, but not all had made use of them to relate to God through faith in the coming Messiah, the long-promised King. Jesus had, then, good reason to be concerned for the crowd. The fact that they were milling around him did not mean that they were concerned to enter his kingdom. What is more, their opportunities to do so were running out.

There is a parallel situation today pertaining to those who have grown up in the Christian church. They have affiliated to it whether by infant baptism, dedication, or adherence, have heard Jesus speak through his preached Word, and have witnessed lives Jesus has transformed, but are yet to hear him, to know him, and to surrender to him. They are in the church, at least in its visible expression, but remain outside the kingdom. They have what

Benjamin Keach calls a *notional knowledge* but they lack a fuller *effective* or *experiential* knowledge suffused with repentance and faith—the *sine qua non* or essential condition of entrance into the kingdom.

This form of Christianity—the churchianity of the unconverted, often found in areas where the church still possesses some vestiges of social standing—is a hangover from the widespread influence of Judeo-Christian values on society. It is a cultural "Christianity" which encourages a modicum of attention to Christianity, but which marginalizes Christ. In it, Christ receives no authentic worship, love, service, or submission. It is a civic religion full of christianese but more akin to a patriotic lobby group for traditional values than to a love affair with Christ and a passion for the spread of his kingdom. This "Christianity" is more about "What's in it for me?" Biblical Christianity, by contrast, attests cultural mores by Scripture, welcomes conviction of sin and the gifts of repentance and faith in Christ, and finds greatest purpose in life in seeking the glory and enjoyment of God by means of service in and through the kingdom of heaven. This does not mean to say that patriotism or traditional values are wrong and to be thrown out—far from it! But they are not to be substituted for Christ or for his gospel. They cannot save souls. Patriotism and traditional values can make us upstanding citizens of society, but they cannot gain us entrance into Christ's kingdom.

If this resonates with you, knowing in the inner recesses of your heart that your respect for Christianity falls far short of surrendering to Christ's claim over your life, then pay particular attention to Christ's parable. He sows the word of the kingdom into your heart as well. As in the case of the crowds, your opportunities for receiving it are decreasing. Not only does the onward march of life ensure this, so does the impending judgment of God on those disregarding Jesus' loving call to come out of the crowd and into the kingdom.

Third, and most culpable of all are those who have gone so far as to profess faith in the Lord Jesus but whose profession of faith turns out to be less than saving faith and lacks the evidence of a life surrendered to Christ. Before dismissing this as too negative, consider that prior to the parable Jesus had warned of this possibility, cautioning us, to use present-day speak, that to profess to be a Christian is not the same as being one. In his Sermon on the Mount, he spoke of the final day,

> Not everyone who says to me, "Lord, Lord," will enter the kingdom of heaven, but the one who does the will of my Father who is in heaven. On that day many will say to me, "Lord, Lord, did we not prophesy in your name, and cast out demons in your name and do many mighty works in your name?" And then will I declare to them, "I never knew you; depart from me, you workers of lawlessness." (Matthew 7:21-23).

Now, in his parable of the sower, Jesus underlines that it is not our words that testify to the authenticity of our Christianity but the bearing of fruit for God's glory (John 15:8). What is more, subsequent events in the ministry of Jesus were to prove very clearly the reality of the false disciple.[9] Thus, the apostle Peter who heard the parable later exhorted his readers to be more diligent to make their calling and election sure (2 Peter 1:10).

Hear the parable then, especially if you suspect this may be true of you. False professors are a possibility in any denomination or congregation. Jesus' parable, specifically the seed landing on rocky ground, teaches us as much. Permit me, though, to reach out in love to those in two scenarios the Lord has laid on my heart. These, it seems to me, can become breeding grounds for false professions of faith.

---

[9] For more on this, see the Afterword.

Consider some generic evangelical churches where low expectations of committed discipleship suit those wanting to profess Christ without the cost of doing so. Specifically, I ponder the impact of churches where there is:

- Minimal acknowledgement of the Lord's Day.
- Low or unstated expectations of church attendance.
- Acceptance of virtually anonymous attendance at worship (especially in megachurches).
- An optional approach to church membership.
- Neglect or patchy exercise of church discipline.

Under such circumstances it is very easy to take the name *Christian* with little personal help or accountability for doing so. This sort of easy-believism or costless discipleship is aided and abetted when church leaderships emphasize numbers attending over rigorous disciples committing. Jesus, though, had little time for the blurring of lines distinguishing the church and the world. Such lines render it comparatively easy for those abandoning their profession of faith to recede back into society, although the successive waves of those continuing to buy into Christianity-lite obscure much of the true picture of what is happening under our noses. If the truth be told, the biblical notion of what is a Christian is at stake in many churches.

Then consider those continental Reformed churches in which false professions can be explained theologically. I refer to the presuming of the regeneration of covenant children. Presumptive regeneration arises from a lopsided view of God's covenant, in which the privileges of relationship with God are stressed at the expense of the responsibilities of repenting and believing. Thus, covenant children and their counterparts (covenant children come of age) are deemed converted simply because they have not openly rejected the faith by the time they have completed "catechism class" (instruction in the Heidelberg Catechism). Either way, presumptive regeneration offers but a mistaken or brittle assurance of salvation and encourages the acceptance of covenant children into the full (communicant) membership of the church as if it were a matter of course. While there is no infallible means of attesting a genuine profession of faith, it is precarious for the spiritual health of the church to assume that because a candidate for profession of faith can answer correctly doctrinal questions that he or she must be regenerate and of Christ's kingdom. Doctrinal questions truly matter, but they do not negate the fundamental question of what Christ means to the candidate personally.

Whereas in generic evangelicalism, the christianese takes more typically the form of a lukewarm, easy-going, minimal commitment to Christ and his church; in Reformed churches impacted by a principled or virtual presumptive regeneration,[10] christianese manifests itself in a joyless devotion to God's law *in lieu* of a humble trust in the perfect righteousness and atoning death of Christ.[11] Theologically orthodox in the main, such folk labor

---

[10] Virtual presumptive regeneration is likely more common these days than a principled presumptive regeneration, and may likely be a hangover from days when the latter was more tenaciously upheld. I refer to scenarios in which presumptive regeneration is denied and yet seems to linger in the presuming that covenant children are saved, in the struggle to accept or to understand the conversion of baptized members and, even more so, the conversion of communicant members previously accepted as full members on the basis of their intellectual affirmation of the doctrinal tenets of the Heidelberg Catechism.

[11] I am not saying that all continental Reformed churches have a distorted view of the Reformed faith and a lopsided view of the covenant, but there is certainly a need in certain circles for a conscious rejection of presumptive regeneration and of a proactive encouragement of a personal faith in Christ and an intimate relationship with God. One hears too many claims in a city like Grand Rapids, Michigan, of people feeling that they only heard the gospel once they left the continental Reformed churches of their upbringing. Since the Heidelberg Catechism is full of the gospel, perhaps they mean by that that the gospel was only applied to them personally as sinners once they got away from churches or individual ministries or leaderships presuming their conversion to Christ. Whichever, I rejoice that they came to know the Lord Jesus, but lament that so many have felt the need to abandon Reformed churches to do so.

under the burden of doing their best to keep the law. Understandably, they fail miserably, succeeding too often in turning off their children to the faith by their inability to emit the life of Christ and the assurance of his love. Those repelled by the legalism can, unless anchored to Christ, rebound into an opposing doctrinal indifferentism or ethical licentiousness. That is not right either but, in West Michigan, it is a dynamic seen too often to be denied.

Allowing for the possibility that some may be truly in Christ but are operating from day-to-day off a distortion of the gospel, I am nevertheless most sensitive to both the reality and plight of the false professor. I was once one, which goes to show that the danger is a matter of the heart and not solely one of generic evangelical practices and continental Reformed theologizing.

Growing up in a Christian home in Wales and weekly attending church, I claimed as an eight-year-old that I had become a Christian. The claim was based on a misunderstanding of what it means to believe the gospel. I took the words of Scripture about faith to refer to a mere mental affirmation of the theological truths of Scripture (Keach's notional knowledge), reasoning that since I did not doubt any of Scripture, I must possess the faith of which Scripture speaks. By the age of fifteen, however, it was obvious that my profession of faith was mistaken. There was, to draw from Jesus' parable of the sower, no spiritual fruit to demonstrate its authenticity. I thus entered a period of much soul-searching and prayer in which God used my head knowledge to convict me of how much I needed to trust personally in Christ for my salvation.

Involved in this conviction was the belief that I could not call on God in sincerity while simultaneously clinging to a profession of faith I knew to be false. God, I became keenly aware, could see through my façade. Thus, I became convinced of the need to be as honest with God as I had become with myself. Such transparency became a key feature of my pursuit of God. Committed to this, God graciously helped me to come clean with him as well as with my family.

Misbehaving one Sunday lunchtime, my father took me to the bedroom. Looking deflated, he calmly began, "I always rejoiced that twenty-five percent of my children know the Lord, but I must say that I am struggling to see the evidence of it." With that he got straight to the point: "Do you love Christ?" Now had Dad asked me whether I was a Christian, I could have palmed him off with some vague answer. But in getting straight to the core of what it means to be a Christian, I saw the kind providence of God. Grasping it with both hands, I answered quietly, "No." My father's face drained of its color. He was seemingly stunned by my straightforwardness. Following a pregnant pause in which neither of us knew quite what to say, he thanked me for being honest. He did not know, though, how the Lord was working in me to bring me to himself. In that moment, a great weight came rolling off me. At no previous time in my life had I been closer to submitting to Christ. The darkest moment in my father's experience of our close relationship was the beginning of a new dawn for me. From then on, I felt free to seek God earnestly and sincerely, hiding nothing from him, and three months later came to true faith in the Lord Jesus.

My story helps explain my burden that false professors would heed Jesus' command to hear his parable. I seek, though, not to superimpose my story on yours, but to put it out there for the sake of those who sense that their profession of faith is spurious and are experiencing the sort of inner turmoil I knew those decades ago. The way through it entails forgoing your original profession of faith in order to cling in faith to Christ. You will not regret facing the issue head on.

My greater concern, however, is for those who lash out at the mere suggestion of the reality of a false profession. One could perhaps understand this if it were to become a frequently beaten drum, but since I only experienced this ire after twenty years of preaching across various Christian traditions and on different continents, and only upon entering into communities exposed to the teaching or assumption of presumptive regeneration, I found the reaction, typified by the complaint, "You are undermining our assurance of salvation!" to be greatly troubling. The charge weighed heavily on me initially. I took it to the Lord and sought counsel from others. The devil beat me up with the charge for months, until God helped me see that it is presumption and not assurance that is that brittle, and that the devil would love nothing more than to put a stop to my arousing of the false professor from his or her sleep of death.

The true disciple by contrast welcomes the opportunity to attest periodically their profession of faith, for their assurance lies not in themselves but in Christ and his promises. It is affirmed by the inner infallible witness of the Holy Spirit and by the evidence of grace (WCF 18:1-2). Circumstances can cause our personal assurance of salvation to fluctuate, yet true assurance is not fragile. It withstands self-examination and is to be distinguished from the false hope of the false professor. His or her carnal presumption rests not on Christ but on self, on good deeds, on church connections, and the like.[12] Are we surprised that it is so brittle?

Do heed, then, Jesus' command to hear his parable. He offers you in love an opportunity to examine whether you are in the kingdom. Don't be alarmed by this. If it turns out that you have entered the kingdom, then the season of self-examination will prove to be a joyful affirmation of what, by grace, you already know. If you conclude that you have professed Christ mistakenly, then, alternatively, Jesus has granted you in love an opportunity to substitute your fake Christianity for him. Only those knowing of

---

[12] Reference to self-examination ought not to be confused with introspection. The former looks to Christ, is therefore extraspective, and is intensive in periods. The latter looks to self, is manically self-focused (to varying degrees), and abidingly so.

Jesus' command to hear the parable but choosing to bury it have cause to fear.

The command to the apostles and true disciples to hear the parable.

Whereas Mark's account of the parable begins with Jesus' directive to hear his parable, Matthew's account tells us that Jesus issued the directive a second time. This time he spoke not to all the crowd but specifically to his disciples as he answers their request for an interpretation of the parable: "Hear the parable of the sower," he begins (Matthew 13:18).

The verb from which Jesus' command originates is the same as the one in Mark's account (ἀκούω), but the mood changes from the present to the aorist (ἀκούσατε, second person plural aorist imperative active). In comparing and contrasting Jesus' two commands, we deduce that whereas Jesus says that all are to keep on hearing the parable, actually listening to what Jesus has to say, Christ's apostles and disciples are to go further. By listening to Jesus they are not only to draw from the parable for their own benefit but are to learn how to interpret correctly what he has to say. Jesus says in effect, "Whereas my command to hear the parable signified that there is no entrance into the kingdom without listening to the Word of the kingdom, my command to you to hear the interpretation signifies that there is no reliable understanding of the ministry of the kingdom where my servants and subjects fail to listen to me." He rebuffs thereby not only those outside the kingdom whose interest in Jesus amounts to no more than a consumerist attitude ("What's in it for me?"), but those in the kingdom who turn ministry into the building and promotion of their own kingdoms or brands, or who empower ministers and ministries intent on doing so.

Note, though, that it was the disciples and not specifically the apostles who asked for the interpretation of the parable(s) (Matthew 13:10; cf., 13:36). The apostles were, of course, disciples of Christ, but not all the disciples were apostles. We assume, therefore, that it was a representation of both apostles and disciples who sought to know how to understand the parable. Both were commanded by Christ to hear the interpretation. The apostles needed to since they were the ones who were going to preach the gospel of the kingdom and to establish churches across the known world. The disciples needed to, not only to understand their responsibility to bear fruit from the ministry of the Word but to appreciate how their witness to Christ would be received by their peers.

Consider in turn the onus resting on the apostles and the disciples.

The apostolate included Simon Peter and Andrew his brother; James and John the sons of Zebedee; Philip and Bartholomew; Thomas and Matthew himself (the tax collector); James the son of Alphaeus, and Thaddaeus; and Simon the Cananaean. In the mystery of providence it also included "Judas Iscariot, who betrayed him" (Matthew 10:4). We shall have more to say of Judas again. As for the remainder of the apostles, Jesus' parable was designed to explain why they received the Word of the kingdom while others had not, and what ministry of the Word looks like. In effect, then, the parable served to further Jesus' mentoring of his proteges.

Throughout their few years together, Jesus mentored his apostles by personal example. He lived among them. They could observe him firsthand (cf., John 1:14; 1 John 1:1). Yet, they were exposed to Jesus not only for the sake of their salvation, but that they might be initiated into ministry. He had already sent them out with instructions as to how they were to minister, but since the time had not yet come for them to go to the nations, they were to avoid the Samaritans and the Gentiles. They were to go only to the lost sheep of the house of Israel, proclaiming to them that the kingdom of heaven is at hand. To demonstrate its arrival they were to heal the sick, raise the dead, cleanse lepers, and cast out demons, just as Jesus had been doing. They were not—contrary to the perception of today's millionaire pastors—to be in the ministry for the money. Rather, they were to preach the Word without distraction (which would also preclude keeping pastors poor), staying only with the honorable, pronouncing peace upon those fitting the bill (Matthew 10:5-15).

Now Jesus sought, through his parable, to introduce his apostles to the next stage of their apprenticeship. Specifically, the parable of the sower taught them:

- Of the focus of their calling, namely, the sowing of the seed of the Word of the kingdom. Whereas the miracles they performed signified the coming of the kingdom, the parable taught the apostles that it would by the sowing of the Word that the kingdom of heaven would spread.

- That they would be opposed by many of their hearers but also by the devil who does all in his power to thwart hearers from entering the kingdom. This lesson built on that which Jesus had already imparted to the apostles, namely, that, "A disciple is not above his teacher, nor a servant above his master. It is enough for the disciple to be like his teacher, and the servant like his master. If they called the master of the house Beelzebub, how much more will they malign those of his household" (Matthew 10:24-25).

- That faithfulness in sowing the seed of the Word trumps successfulness in doing so. No matter the preacher, in endeavoring to minister the Word there will always be those who dismiss it without giving it thought, who show promise in hearing it but in whom the Word comes to nothing, and who smother the Word so that it is has no effect. The apostles would need to expect this, while also remaining confident that the seed would, in God's timing and choice of place, reap a harvest of fruit.

Long ago, the office of apostle fulfilled its purpose, as did the signs of the apostles (Acts 5:12; Romans 15:18-19; 2 Corinthians 12:12). Even before the canon of Scripture was complete, the signs affirming Jesus' arrival were becoming a phenomenon of history. The great salvation, writes the author of Hebrews, "*was* declared at first by the Lord, and it *was* attested to us by those who heard, while God also *bore witness* by signs and wonders and various miracles and by gifts of the Holy Spirit distributed according to his will" (2:3-4 [italics inserted]).

This does not mean to say that God cannot and does not work miracles today. The many false or trumped up claims today of miracles among those more nostalgic for the powers of the early adulthood of the church, should not blind us in unbelief to the reality of miraculous phenomena. While there are particular incidents experienced across the world, it is noteworthy that the supernatural is prevalent where the Scriptures are unavailable, disallowed, or untranslated. In such instances the phenomena serve to convince those without the Scriptures of the authenticity of Christ and the veracity of the gospel. It would be mistaken, however, to regard such phenomena as a continuation of those forms of special revelation predating the canon of Scripture. Today's verifiable miracles suit more generally the category of God's prevenient grace (the grace that goes before salvation). They ready those without the Scriptures to receive the written and living Word, by opening otherwise closed minds and hearts to Christianity. It is as if God uses the miracles to override Satan's attempt to put the elect beyond his reach. Miracles, however, as distinctive signs of the apostles, faded into history with the closure of the office at the end of the apostolic era.

Given all this, the parable of the sower is no longer used to mentor apostles. It is, however, very relevant to those of us called to preach, for by preaching apostolic doctrine we stand on the shoulders of the apostles. The continuity of the church's ministry lies, then, not in the temporary performance of miracles but in the ongoing preaching of the Word. Through the preaching of Christ, ministers of the Word build today on the foundation of the apostles (cf., Ephesians 2:20). But here is the irony. Many claim in the miraculous a fallacious continuity with the apostles while, simultaneously, cutting themselves adrift from a biblically legitimized continuity with the apostles by their distortion, dilution, or downplaying of the preached Word.

Since the canon of Scripture is complete, there is little justification for this. The abandonment has had a devastating effect on the strength of the church. The dearth of biblical knowledge and reliable biblical exposition in the pulpits has impacted most negatively the spiritual maturity of those in the pews. In turn, the dearth of biblical knowledge in the pews has limited appetites for the exposition of the Word. The resultant decline of pulpit ministry has succeeded in shrinking further our appetites for the Word. Unless checked, the downward spiral in biblical literacy goes on and on.

Due reflection of the context and content of Jesus' parable of the sower is one way we can call for a return in worship to the ministry of the Word on its own terms. The Word speaks fundamentally about God's glory not man's, and about Christ's kingdom and not ours. Therefore, ministers who truly belong to the kingdom of heaven, whose ministries and lives are surrendered to the reign of Christ, have a responsibility to challenge current trends in preaching. Dumbed down, seeker-loaded,[13] success-oriented

---

[13] I prefer the term "seeker-loaded" to "seeker-friendly" ministry, since criticism of "seeker-friendly" ministry can be heard to oppose welcoming seekers into the

ministries are long overdue being reformed. Gone must be the belief that the exposition of the Word will not accomplish that which can be achieved by a man-centered, touchy-feely, anecdotal (sound-biting), or need-focused preaching. Where a lack of trust or satisfaction in the purposes of God has set in, repentance is warranted and a fresh surrendering of our fears, our personal branding, and our kingdoms to Christ.

I am not advocating the sort of pulpit ministry which is all about faithfulness with little concern for fruitfulness. Where the delivery is antiquarian, without liveliness or authority, omitting attention to those outside the kingdom, and influencing a general aimlessness of congregational life, it is difficult to swallow diatribes about the problems of "contemporary churches." A handful gathered in a subdued atmosphere, speaking a language of worship from another age, with unchurched visitors few and far between, and congregations prone to split over secondary issues in any given chapter of its history, is hardly a compelling case against all things contemporary.

In the parable of the sower Jesus indicates that there will be fruit from the ministry of the Word. Those ministering in the apostolic tradition are legitimately concerned to see it appear. But the success (read fruit) Jesus had in mind arises from the exposition

---

worship of the church family and the making of our sermons as accessible as possible within the parameters of biblical exposition. This is not what troubles any self-respecting critic of "seeker-friendly ministry." Rather, the best critics are concerned to uphold the divinely regulated worship of the Lord's Day, which, second to focusing on God, is designed by him to equip the saints for ministry. While, then, we preach the gospel in worship to saints and non-saints alike, we do not so focus on visiting seekers as to malnourish the saints who are under training. Instead, we strengthen the members through the preached Word so that they are equipped to engage seekers and non-seekers alike during the week, and we lay on opportunities within the broader life of the church to help facilitate this engagement.

of the Word and not from a deviation from it. The fruit pertains to godliness and to committed discipleship and not necessarily to mass audiences or even to numbers of professing converts. That said, those ministers touting their faithfulness without evidence of fruitfulness, would do well to ask themselves whether their cultural packaging of church life is hindering accessibility to the Word, whether their preferences unaddressed in the Word have become so elevated as to undermine those clear principles of the Word, and whether their churches are reaching out relevantly in obedience to the Great Commission and by means of the Word. If they are not, then their faithfulness is as much in question as their fruitfulness, for the Great Commission is, as the name discloses, an imperative from Christ not an option we can take or leave.

Clearly, then, the apostles, given their strategic significance in the spread of the kingdom and their establishment of churches across the known world, needed to hear Christ's parable. But, so did the disciples who were with the apostles in asking for its interpretation. They were not officebearers of Christ as were the apostles, but Jesus had reasons as to why they, too, must take in the parable and its interpretation.

First, Jesus was indicating to his followers the fundamental significance of the Word. The Word not only calls us to enter the kingdom of heaven, it is the constitution by which citizens of the kingdom live. More than that, it is the means by which his disciples grow in submission to his reign and conformity to his image. Just prior to his crucifixion and with his departure from earth in mind, Christ prayed to his Father that he would sanctify his disciples in the truth, adding "your word is truth" (John 17:17). Essentially, then, Christ's command that his disciples hear the parable and its interpretation was a directive that they become, as we might say today, people of the book. True disciples are known for being just that. They understand the parable more than they understand those claiming to be disciples, who:

- Habitually undermine its authority.
- Interpret away its clear meaning.
- Forever claim the ministry of the Word goes on too long.

What, we may ask, would Jesus think of professing disciples who show little interest in the Word of God? Would he automatically side with those for whom no sermon can be too short? Or who object on his day to hearing a second message or to attending a Bible study as part of an evening sacrifice of praise (cf., the spirit of Psalm 134:1-3)? Hardly!

Second, Jesus directs his disciples to hear the parable because to them was given the capacity of understanding the mysteries of the kingdom. Think about his parables for a moment. Although he used down-to-earth pictures all could understand, they confounded the impenitent crowds. Jesus thereby dispelled the myth, so liable to make a comeback in days of biblical illiteracy, that all it takes for the crowds to understand the Word and to come flooding into the church and into the kingdom is the dumbing down of sermons. No matter how simple the language of the preacher, there is no comprehension of the Word of the kingdom without the illumination of the King. Thus, in interpreting the parable, Jesus gives his disciples the very understanding he commands them to have. The apostle Paul later referred to this illumination in terms of the need of God-given spiritual discernment (cf., 1 Corinthians 2:14).

Akitela, a lady of the Turkana tribe in Kenya, illustrates very well that the mysteries of the kingdom are divinely given. Entering the church for the first time, hearing an exposition of God's Word, through translation, which was directed predominantly to the Lord's people, she nevertheless came forward spontaneously at the end of the sermon to ask for prayer that she might heed the call of Joshua to forsake the gods of the surrounding nations for the Lord God of Israel (Joshua 24:1-28). If anyone had justifiable complaint for not understanding the Word, it was Akitela. She had been under the sway of the witch doctor, but by the power of God working through the Word translated into her mother tongue, she knelt uninvited at the front of the church, and oblivious to the congregation sought prayer for the strength to forsake the witch doctor for Christ.

Akitela's response to the Word pointedly teaches us that Christ's disciples today are not to buy into the fallacy that the truth is intellectually rather than spiritually discerned. You can have highly intelligent people with the finest educations who just do not get the message, and those like Akitela with everything going against her to preclude her from receiving the Word, who nevertheless take it in and act on it. We do not, then, subject ministers of the Word to undue pressure to produce sermons which evade the mind. To do so, is to rob those with the spiritual capacity and desire to glean from the Word, and to empower plaintiffs who have neither.

We would understand much of this, if, as disciples of Christ, we heed his command to hear the parable. Jesus intends us not to skim-read it but to study it prayerfully, taking it to heart and understanding how weighty is its challenge. Let us avoid appearing before Jesus someday, unable to look him in the eye should he ask us how we heard his parable. Rather, let us give our attention to it. It reminds us of the need to be in the kingdom, and, if we are in it, to be fully in. No holding back! I speak to myself most of all.

STUDY QUESTIONS: SESSION THREE

1. Why is Matthew's Gospel especially suited to a study of Jesus' parable of the sower?

2. What differences can you list between members of the crowd and subjects of the kingdom? How may we discern these differences without falling into judgmentalism?

3. The crowds were responsible for not understanding the mysteries of the kingdom. How so? What implications does that have for our reviews of faithful preaching today?

4. From what you have learned thus far, what makes a ministry successful in the eyes of the world but not so in the eyes of God? And what makes a ministry a failure in the eyes of the world and even, perhaps, in the eyes of the church, but not so in the eyes of God?

5. Discuss the differences you perceive between hearing the words of a sermon and listening to it.

6. Could Christ say of you, "blessed are *your* eyes, for they see, and *your* ears, for they hear"? If so, in what ways have you observed that to be true?

Prayer: Father, thank you for sending Christ to establish the kingdom, and for the grace given us to listen to what he says of it. Help us to distinguish the christianese of the crowd from the Christianity of the kingdom, to leave the one for the other, and to be assured that our eyes and ears are blessed. In Christ's name we pray. Amen.

In preparation for chapter four, read: Isaiah 55:6-13; 1 Corinthians 2:1-16.

PART TWO

"A SOWER WENT OUT TO SOW"

Matthew 13:1-8, 18-23

4.

THE SEED ALONG THE PATH

[3] And he told them many things in parables, saying: "A sower went out to sow. [4] And as he sowed, some seeds fell along the path, and the birds came and devoured them."

[18] Hear then the parable of the sower: [19] When anyone hears the word of the kingdom and does not understand it, the evil one comes and snatches away what has been sown in his heart. This is what was sown along the path.

Matthew 13:3-4, 18-19

[3] "Listen! A sower went out to sow. [4] And as he sowed, some seed fell along the path, and the birds came and devoured it."

[14] The sower sows the word. [15] And these are the ones along the path, where the word is sown: when they hear, Satan immediately comes and takes away the word that is sown in them.

Mark 4:3-4, 14-15

[5] A sower went out to sow his seed. And as he sowed, some fell along the path and was trampled under foot, and the birds of the air devoured it.

[11] Now the parable is this: The seed is the word of God. [12] The ones along the path are those who have heard; then the devil comes and takes away the word from their hearts, so that they may not believe and be saved.

Luke 8:5, 11-12

Evidently, Jesus' parable was relevant to all before him—to his apostles and disciples as also to the crowds, to those inside as well as outside his kingdom. The parable, however, mainly focuses on those outside. We have identified a couple of reasons for this.

First, Jesus was concerned to mentor his subjects (the apostles and disciples), affording them a realistic view of ministry. He explains to them why not all come to repentance and faith and to an understanding of the mysteries of the kingdom. He was functioning in effect as the master physician of souls, who, surrounded by trainee physicians, with the disciples in the spectator gallery, performs an operation on the souls in the crowd before him. The procedure aimed to show the apostles and disciples how they were to make spiritual diagnoses once Jesus had returned to heaven. Accordingly, Jesus, with scalpel in hand, begins to cut through the layers of skin and tissue before him to get to the issues of the heart.

How relevant this is to the spiritual oversight of churches today. Ministers and elders, serving in the apostolic tradition, would do better to treat their meetings as surgical consultations aiming at identifying the causes, symptoms, and cures of the souls under their charge than as customer service departments seeking to satisfy consumer complaints. Congregants are not clients to be satisfied ("The customer is always right!") but are souls in need of healing and of health. Christ's authentic and maturing disciples appreciate this and, when walking with the Lord, support the minister's faithful exposition of the Word and the eldership's spiritual oversight of the congregation. They know that while biblical exposition may not be in vogue and may not grow the church numerically to the degree that the anecdotal preaching does down the road, it is required by the Word, is pleasing to God, is for the best of the people, and heals hearts, church families, and communities.

Second, Jesus sought to share with the crowds the reasons for which they remained impenitent and unbelieving, and why God was inaugurating his judgment against them. Whether they understood him or not, his readiness to allow the Word, as a scalpel, to cut deep into the souls of his hearers separated him, the Old Testament prophets, and the apostles (in their preaching to come), from the false prophets, the fake Messiahs, the pseudo-apostles, and the men-pleasers of history. Whereas the latter preach what people want to hear, Jesus preached what the people needed. His doing so would in time thin out his followers, but those trusting their lives to him would experience the salvation, and the spiritual health and growth he offered.

If the church is to be strengthened, we need a revival of this sort of preaching. It goes without saying that ministry in Jesus' name must be loving, but it is a caricature of Jesus to insist it must always be encouraging or tender. Jesus' default position was to speak to his hearers tenderly, yet his love frequently required him to speak forthrightly and directly, leaving the chips to fall where they may. Faithful ministers of the Word understand this, but not all who hear them do. Such ministers may well have to resist the myth that Christ only speaks through preachers when their messages are tender and comforting. This flies not only in the face of Paul's description of the use of Scripture in 2 Timothy 3:16 which includes reproof, correction, and training in righteousness, but also in the face, for example, of Christ's letter to the ministers (angels) of the first-century churches of Asia Minor (Revelation 2–3). He threatens to remove the Ephesian church; to war against some in the church at Pergamum; to bring sickness, tribulation, and death upon those in the church at Thyatira following the prophetess Jezebel; to visit the church in Sardis as a thief (presumably to steal the lampstand); and to reprove and discipline those whom he loved in the church at Laodicea (Revelation 2:5, 16, 22-23, 3:3, 19). So, to resist the myth, ministers of the Word, while seeking the balance of Scripture, risk being misunderstood and even opposed, especially when the Word is processed by hearers emotionally rather than biblically.

To draw once more from the medical analogy, we naturally prefer the band aid to invasive surgery, but it is the surgery which holds out the greater promise of healing. Recall the complaint of the Lord of hosts against the prophets and priests of Jeremiah's day: "They have healed the wound of my people lightly, saying, 'Peace, peace,' when there is no peace" (Jeremiah 6:14; cf., 8:11). Thus, when we hear a minister of the Word seeking to speak forth Jesus' words after him, we need a basic trust of that ministry, uncomfortable though it may be. If we give our consent to a surgeon to cut us open, to meddle with our innards, to sow us up again, and to set us on the path of healing, why is it so difficult for us to allow a called, qualified, and trained servant of God to use the Word to diagnose and to address our life-threatening diseases? Is the temporary pain we feel in conviction of sin really so unbearable that we would permit a surgeon to perform an operation on us to correct a physical malady before we allow a minister to correct one that is spiritual? Perhaps we prefer the prolongation of this life to the preparation necessary to the one to come.

Thus, with the apostles (and the disciples) watching on, Jesus now addresses the crowd in parables. It makes sense that he should do so, for as he stated—ironically on the occasion he called Matthew to himself—"Those who are well have no need of a physician, but those who are sick" (Matthew 9:12). But there is another irony. Jesus begins his parable of the sower addressing the men and women on whom the Word of the kingdom has no effect. In other words, he sets out by addressing those on which healing, as things stand, will prove undesirable. He refers to those whose hearts are, like the seed landing along the path, well-nigh impenetrable.

THE REALITIES OF SOWING

Both the parable and the interpretation begin with the sower (vv. 3-4, 18). Jesus tells us that the sower is the one who dispenses the Word of God. For centuries this had been true of the Old

Testament prophets. They had sown the seed of God's Word by their divinely revealed "forthtelling" ("Thus says the LORD . . .") as also by their foretelling (prediction of the future). As Messiah, Jesus stood in continuity with them, declaring as a prophet the Word of God. Yet, he was also discontinuous from them, for unlike the prophets, Jesus was, as the divine Messiah, also the content of the divine revelation he proclaimed. Accordingly, the parable of the sower is, in the immediate context, about his personal dispensing of the Word of the kingdom. He, ultimately, is the sower who spreads his seed. Yet, in his sowing, Jesus also had in mind his apostles to whom he would commit the responsibility of sowing the Word over a field stretching across Jerusalem, Judea, Samaria, and unto the ends of the known world. We who preach stand in turn upon their shoulders.

The sowing of the seed of the Word is a specific calling the prophets, Christ, the apostles, and ministers of the Word share in common. This calling from God Jesus' parable addresses in terms of three realities.

The reality of sowing.

Jesus begins his parable, "A sower went out to sow" (Matthew 13:3). Now, we would expect the sower to, for that is what sowers do, and what is in fact what Jesus was doing as he embarked on telling his parable. It is as if he now raises his arm to scatter the seed of the Word over the crowd (aka, the field). After all, Jesus was first and foremost a preacher rather than the miracle-worker or exorcist for which he is often taken (cf., Mark 1:38). In fact, preaching was as essential to Jesus' ministry as sowing is to horticultural farming.

The apostles were to remember this. Having earlier displayed the signs of the kingdom how easy it would be for them to forget that, chiefly, they were to sow the seed of the Word. The signs, although life-changing for those benefiting from them, were but intended to create a hearing for the preaching of the kingdom. Neither the apostles nor the crowds were, then, to become so preoccupied with the signs as if they were ends in themselves. The signs came first and were followed by the Word precisely to authenticate the arrival of the kingdom and the saving work of Jesus. The signs of the apostles were temporary, but they succeeded in perpetuating an audience for the preaching of Christ that has stretched down to the present.

If preaching takes precedence over the authentic historic signs of the apostles, it is certain that it has top billing over the fallacious claims of would-be apostles today. These do so much to bring the church of Christ into disrepute. Yet, others of us need to recall that preaching also has priority over administration, over writing, and even over pastoral work. Pastoral work done well is incredibly necessary for it helps to bring home the preaching to the hearer in the particular details of his or her life, but it does not supplant preaching. Administration cannot be avoided, but paperwork plays third fiddle to preaching and to pastoral work. A writing ministry can spread the gospel and build up the wider church, but it does not justify the neglect of the people to whom we are called and who, typically, pay our salaries.

Our call as preachers is to do all we can to preach, and that includes study, prayer, and the delivery of sermons. If, then, we occupy a position on the ministerial staff of the church or in a ministry in which the dispensing of God's Word (in one form or another) is not front and center, then we need to think again. Either we must change our position to get back to our true calling, or we must accept that our calling is not that of preacher of the Word and adopt a job title other than minister or pastor. "Church administrator," for example, would be more fitting than "executive pastor." If the executive pastor is essentially involved in dispensing the Word, then the adjective "executive" needs to be dropped.

The reality of the seed.

As the sower concerns himself with the seed, so the preacher concerns himself with the Word. We are not called to preach our personal stories, although some anecdotes are helpful in so far as they illustrate the Word. Neither are we called to preach politics, although the Word may be applied to the political sphere.[1] Nor, furthermore, are we called to preach our opinions, although they are needed in various places of uncertain interpretation, as also in the application. Rather, in preaching, the Word is to predominate. After all, it is our sole authority. "If we do not possess a positive appetite for the Word," warns Arthur Skevington Wood, "then we are not meant to be preachers. For it is not anything other than the word that we're called to preach."[2]

Jesus describes the Word in the context of the parable as "the word of the kingdom" (v. 19). Indeed, it is the notion of the kingdom which shapes a true perception of preaching. By its very emphases the kingdom teaches us that preaching should be:

- *God-centered.* We preach Christ's kingdom and not our own! The goal of preaching is that God is glorified through the coming of men and women, boys and girls under the reign of Jesus.

- *Gospel-focused.* We preach repentance toward God on account of the dysfunction created by our own "kingdoms," and faith in Christ for entrance into his kingdom which drew near through his incarnation (Matthew 4:17).

---

[1] For more on this subject, see Tim J.R. Trumper, *Preaching and Politics: Engagement without Compromise* (Eugene, OR: Wipf and Stock, 2009).
[2] Quoted in *Gathered Gold: A Treasury of Quotations for Christians*, compiled by John Blanchard (Welwyn, Hertfordshire, England: Evangelical Press, 1984), 236.

- *Life-transforming.* The preacher declares not only how to get into the kingdom of heaven but how we are to live out its countercultural lifestyle (e.g., Matthew 5–7).

- *Mission-minded.* We desire as preachers to see the reign of Christ spread over the lives of others, even unto the ends of both earth and time.

Where these emphases are not prominent from the pulpit, then church attendees are not hearing preaching. They are receiving something other than the Word of the kingdom.

The reality of the sequence.

Notice in verse 19 where Jesus interprets the meaning of the first soil, that when the seed of the Word is snatched away, it is snatched away *from the heart.* This implies that while the preacher aims at the mind, his goal is to reach the heart. It is for this reason, to quote seventeenth-century pastor Richard Baxter, that we "screw the truth into men's minds." After all, it must be like "well-driven nails" (Ecclesiastes 12:11 [NKJV]). Just as nails go through one substance to fasten to another, so the Word must go through the mind to fasten God's truth to the heart. Accordingly, we neither bypass the mind to get to the heart, nor in preaching do we stop at the mind, thereby leaving the heart untouched. The former inadequacy we identify as emotionalism, the latter as intellectualism.

Jesus had neither in mind. He envisions his apostles establishing a tradition of preaching which informs the mind but pierces the heart. It does so, first with conviction of sin then with the comfort of Christ. Accordingly, Jesus assumes that preaching undertaken in his name will be bold and unafraid of being outspoken. As Baxter put it, "If a hardened heart is to be broken, it is not stroking but striking that must do it."[3] The striking must be done in love for sure, but a ministry that always opts to stroke or to smooth rather than to strike (even when the text calls for striking) will not accomplish much. The pews will likely fill up with crowds looking to feel good about themselves, but the spiritual growth of their souls will be negligible. Either the crowds gathered will have a good representation of intellectuals who tolerate a disconnect between their knowledge and application of Scripture, or a good representation of counselees who soak in the application but know next to nothing about the Scriptures. Jesus calls his servants to a balanced ministry that aims at the mind in order to get to the heart, informing the former to transform the latter.

THE RESPONSIBILITIES OF HEARING

Jesus says that if the seed is being sown—which is to say, that if the Word is being faithfully preached, and yet we remain outside of Christ's kingdom, the problem is ours and not the preacher's. In other words, there is something amiss with our hearts. After all, their condition determines how we respond to the Word.

So far as the scenario of the seed landing along the path is concerned, Jesus discerns two problems.

The hearer understands and yet does not understand the Word.

Unless a person is illiterate, mentally challenged, or has no copy of the Scriptures in their own language, there is no *practical reason* why the Word of God cannot be understood. Although there are words used which are not in our everyday vocabulary (e.g., propitiation, atonement, justification, sanctification, or glorification, etc.), we have plenty of tools available to understand their meaning.

---

[3] Quoted in *A Puritan Golden Treasury*, compiled by I. D. E. Thomas, reprint ed. (Carlisle, PA: The Banner of Truth Trust, 1989), 222.

Likewise, if we use a version of the Bible with archaic English which is to us as comprehensible to us as gobbledygook, then we need to find an alternative, word-for-word (formal-equivalent) translation of the Scriptures to use, such as the English Standard Version or New King James Version. We also have study Bibles galore from which we can glean much useful information (e.g., the Reformation Study Bible).

What is more, there is no *theological reason* either why the Word cannot be understood. We believe the Scriptures to be clear in those matters necessary for our salvation. States the WCF: ". . . those things which are necessary to be known, believed, and observed for salvation, are so clearly propounded and opened in some place of scripture or other, that not only the learned, but the unlearned in a due use of the ordinary means, may attain unto a sufficient understanding of them" (1:7). It follows, then, that the hearer of the Word is able to understand it intellectually (that is to say, with the mind). He or she knows what is being said.

What is lacking, as we saw at the end of the last chapter, is the spiritual understanding. The same mind which perceives the meaning of the words used is, naturally, darkened by the inherited effects of the Fall of our first parents and by personal sin (original and actual). Left to ourselves, we fail to grasp the spiritual weight and application of the words the preacher uses. Consequently, we do not automatically receive the Word.

Recall that by nature the hearer has no spiritual interest in Holy Scripture. We may have some fascination with this piece of narrative, that selection of poetry, or the preacher's style of delivery, but the interest is other than spiritual (how it profits the soul). Perhaps the only reason we go to worship is because dad or mom expected us to be there, or because a sense of decency kept us from revolting against the practice of attending.

Neither have we by nature a spiritual interest in the kingdom of heaven. We may be intrigued as to how Christ has a kingdom that is neither political nor geographical, but, left to ourselves, we do not press upon God that we may enter it. Quite the opposite, we sit in judgment on the Word, finding reasons not to heed the call to repent and to trust in Christ for admission. Since criticism of the Holy Scriptures makes our hubris blatantly obvious, the preacher oftentimes becomes the scapegoat. He may have faithfully urged entrance into the kingdom, yet he is taken to task for erring in some comparatively trivial detail, for man loves, as Jesus said, to swat gnats and to swallow camels (Matthew 23:24)!

Naturally, as preachers we must do what we can to help our hearers. As we get to know them, we tailor our messages to their spiritual needs and our series to their capacities. We acquiesce in supplying information for the weekly bulletin such as the reading, text, and sermon outlines. Some congregations project them onto screens. We think up relevant sermon illustrations to illuminate its principles, offer *Q's and A's* about the sermons, or agree to sermon discussion classes. Following the service, we upload sermons online so that they can be heard a second time. Yet, no matter how much we may help the hearer, we ought always to recall that the truth is spiritually discerned. If we forget that, we'll end up, if we are not careful, dumbing down the truth, or even compromising it to make it palatable. Along the way, we contradict the perspicuity (clarity) of Scripture, and empower the unregenerate in their evasion of the truth as revealed in it.

I fear this is happening somewhat where the sermon is replaced by power-point presentations, interviews, mimes or dances. Instead of giving ourselves as leaders and congregants to prayer for the effectiveness of the ministry of the Word, there is abroad a buying into our current saturation with entertainment and the inevitable anti-intellectualism it has bred (think of Neil Postman's title *Amusing Ourselves to Death* [1985]). Jesus' parable calls us, then, to return to a more discerning evaluation of responses to the ministry of the Word. Where there is an habitual lack of understanding of the Word, hearers have either not received the Spirit and thus remain in the darkness prevailing outside of Christ's kingdom, or they have the Spirit and his illumination but are in the process of backsliding and are experiencing accordingly diminished powers of perception. Thus, the truth of God's Word is not as clear to them as it might be.

The hearer possesses and yet does not possess the Word.

Despite the protestations of those claiming not to understand, the preached Word somehow reaches the hearer's heart. After all, self-defense mechanisms are fallible. Says Jesus, the Word is "sown in his heart" (v. 19). The problem lies, then, not in the Word but in the hearer. He or she does not let it grow in the heart. His or her heart is, says Jesus, like a well-beaten path running aside a wheat field. It is hard, barren, and exposed.

The path is *hard* in the sense that it is dry, arid, and baked by the Middle Eastern sun. The seed lands on the concrete-like surface. There it lies visible to the eye. Soon it is crushed under the feet and hooves of the man and beast creating the path. Likewise, our hearts can be well-worn and hardened by repeated rejection of the Word. The hardening occurs under the influence of a long disobedience in the wrong direction. Having allowed ourselves to become distracted by the convenient busyness of life, our feelings toward God become desensitized. Our resultant callousness is explained by our habitual ignoring of God and his truth.

We call this phenomenon "gospel hardening." Jesus' statement that the seed is sown in the heart reminds us, however, that some seed falling along the path lands in its cracks. He says in effect, that all but those with the most seared of consciences, who have blasphemed the Holy Spirit, retain inlets into their hearts. Through these the seed of the Word finds entrance. Yet, instead of affording space for the seed of the Word to grow, the person with the hardened heart does all in his or her power to ensure that it does not take root there.

The path is also *barren*. Nothing grows on it. The feet and hooves kill off any chance the fresh seed has of growth. Much rain is needed to moisten the ground, but once the seed has been washed away or crushed under foot or hoof, the rain has no effect. There must first be a diversion of traffic from the path, a cultivation of the path, and the sowing of further seed, if the path is to become part of the fruitful soil. Likewise, the hearts of hearers need quiet and rest, a chance to get alone with God and to meditate on his Word. Distractions must be put aside, the Word heard afresh, the heart made available to hear from God. Only under such circumstances does the seed of the Word have an opportunity to soak in the rain of the Holy Spirit and to bear fruit like the good soil.

Since the path is barren it is also *exposed*. With no growth on it, and no possibility of the seed taking root in the soil, the seed is vulnerable. Suffice it to say, that the Word quickly goes to waste, for the heart is liable to negative outside influences. These influences leave minds disinterested, prone to a carnal version of ADHD. Some such hearers grew up in the church but attend in body only, and some remain formally committed to the church but value church as but a social institution. Their minds cannot stay with the Word. Under the Word, they wander over the week past or the week to come. Such "hearers" appear to have no contention with either the preacher or the Word he preaches. This is because they are not listening to the minister. They are, then, too lifeless to pushback, whether mentally or verbally. They neither speak of the kingdom nor make any movement toward it. Try to get a spiritual conversation going with them and the attempt falls flat. There is neither positive response nor negative rebuttal. There is no traction either way. There is just nothing. Wrote J. C. Ryle, "Truth seems to have no more effect on their hearts than water on a stone."[4]

THE RESULTS OF THE WORD

God, we have noted before, promises that his Word does not go out in vain nor return to him empty or without effect (Isaiah 55:10). Yet, if we had only the seed that lands on the pathway to go by, we may be forgiven for thinking that the Lord is not true to his Word or that the prophet Isaiah failed to "forthtell" the Lord's Word correctly. But, of course, the Lord is always true to his Word and the prophet in communicating it was carried along by the Spirit (2 Peter 1:21). Which goes to say that God has his purposes even for the seed that is trampled underfoot or which the birds snatch away. The destroyed or lost seed vindicates in due time God's judgment of the hardened and reminds other hearers to make better use of the Word preached.

Consider the two scenarios Jesus mentions.

The Word is trampled.

The trampling of the seed is brought out in Luke's account of the parable: "As the sower sowed, some fell along the path and was trampled under foot" (Luke 8:5). Evidently, the seed had no time to grow before it was crushed. Such trampling happens in the spiritual realm by acts of omission and commission.

Acts of omission include the want of the reading and rereading of Scripture and of prayer. God has scattered the seed through the spread of his Word, but our neglect of the Word results in its marginalization from our lives. How many unused Bibles, for example, are discovered in estate sales and end up in secondhand

---

[4] J. C. Ryle, *Expository Thoughts on Matthew*, first published 1856 (Carlisle, PA: The Banner of Truth Trust, 1986), 143.

stores? They are sad testimonies to lives lived without passion to know God and to hear what he has to say. The Bible may be an older edition and design, but the pages have not been cracked open, nor then, we may fairly assume, has prayer been offered for divine illumination as to its meaning and application. The owner may have been to church periodically, perhaps at Christmas and Easter, to funerals and weddings, but there has been no follow-up with the minister or consideration of his message of a hell to be shunned and a heaven to be gained. This type of hearer is content to come and go from worship at will, oblivious to the divinely appointed role of the minister of the Word as God's ambassador. He is charged with proclaiming Christ's command that we repent and believe the gospel of the kingdom.

Acts of commission in trampling the Word are worse. The hearer hears the Word preached but does all in his or her power to rid himself of its message. He or she takes active steps to ensure that the command to repent and the invitation to believe do not take root within. Such hearers are content where they are at, and, therefore, they set about drowning out the message even as it is preached.

The most obvious example of this I recall is from my days as a teenager in Wales. A few of us went on Sunday evenings to hold a short service in a hospital ward. As soon it became clear what the elder was speaking about, a lady lying in one of the beds with her eyes shut, thinking the voice was coming from the television, burst out, "Switch him off! Switch him off!" Her reaction to the gospel was more lamentable overall than it was surprising and amusing in the moment. She was giving, however, but vocal expression to what many of the hardened think within.

And not only outside the church. Some, under the pretext that the sermon is boring read the bulletin, others do their shopping lists, others find cause to leave the worship service. They are present bodily on the church premises, but that is about it. Their "worship" is an affront to God, for they fail to recognize that God is *GOD*, which is why they underplay the responsibility of hearing his holy Word. Far from feeling guilty about this, such hearers often lack respect in worship and appear entirely oblivious to the account that they must one day give for what they do in this life with the Word.

The proactive trampling of the Word can be very visible. I think back to a funeral I took. The deceased had been brought up in a Christian home but from his teens had "sown his wild oats." So far as was known he had died that way. Since he died unexpectedly, he had not planned a funeral. What seemed certain is that he would not have wanted a Christian funeral and in all good conscience I could not have given him one. But the children, unaware of how God's Word can be trampled, and the ex-wife careless as to that possibility, insisted that the projected photos of the deceased, set to rock music, follow the service rather than precede it. I had hoped that God's Word would have the last say at the funeral, for which reason I had suggested the photos be shown before the service.

God granted me the courage to depict and then to gently debunk from Scripture the declared philosophy of life of the deceased. Long ago, Jesus had famously anticipated it: "Eat drink and be merry, for tomorrow we die" (Luke 12:19). The depiction was done in love and with the agreement of the man's mother. "Don't preach him into heaven!" she pled. I was not of a mind to, but was so touched to know we were on the same page, and to this day laud her for her courage. As the message went forth, you could cut the atmosphere with a knife. I felt vibes of love from the Lord's people as they listened soberly, doubtlessly praying for the effectiveness of the Word. But I also sensed strong resistance from the friends of the deceased. You could feel the emotional walls going up the more that was said of the pitfalls of life without Christ.

In mingling following the service, the conflicting vibes were still there to be felt. One comment, though, sticks in my mind, and illustrates the trampling of the seed. Defying death and the Judgment by her joviality, the ex-wife loudly proclaimed nearby how good it was to end with the photos and the music. Her "ex," she pronounced, would have loved that. Whether she said it or not to make a dig at me as God's representative on that occasion, is immaterial. My only response was to hang my head, feeling great heaviness of heart for both the deceased and his ex-spouse. The seed sown was being willfully crushed under her feet.

If you are as inclined to trample God's Word, it is certain that your heart will become as dry, barren, and exposed as the path to which Jesus refers. It is also certain that your heart will need as much plowing up as the path, if the seed of the Word is to take root within you. Don't wait for God to plow up your heart through deeply humbling and heart-wrenching crises. He may permit these, either to open your heart to the Word, or to demonstrate its hardness by the bitterness it vents under difficult circumstances. Those spiritually affected for good by such crises give up trampling the Word, for the written Word (Scripture) and the living Word (Christ) become a lifeline to them. In the subsequent softening, God gently sows the seed of the Word into the heart he has pried open. In time the fruit appears. The miracle of grace is wonderful to behold.

God in mercy calls you to till the soil of your heart. Listen to the prophet Hosea: "Break up your fallow ground, for it is time to seek the Lord" (Hosea 10:12). In effect, he tells you to get serious with God. Crack open that dusty Bible, asking him to plant the seed of the Word deep into your heart. He'll answer you by first causing shoots of repentance and faith to grow from the Word sown. That isn't what you want to hear, but it is an eternity better than the further hardening of your heart which inevitably follows on from yet another rejection of God's Word. I implore you, then, not to let your heart become impenetrable. By doing so, you store up wrath for the day of judgment and become an example to others of how not to respond to God's Word.

The Word is snatched away.

In Matthew's account Jesus speaks alternatively of the birds coming and devouring the seed (v. 4). This makes sense. Of all the seed sown in the field, the seed along the path lies visible to the birds and is easily plucked from the ground. Such plucking guarantees the waste of the seed.

In thinking on this, my mind goes to the grave of my father-in-law. Although he was buried in March 2014, no one could have imagined that in a cemetery covered in thick grass his grave would have lain bare these years later. To remedy the situation the cemetery authorities laid fresh topsoil, maintained a mesh over the grave, and repeatedly reseeded it. But the grave continued until recently to stand out as a rectangular patch of dirt. No one seems to know why, nor to have had a solution for it. The only clue to the phenomenon has been the bird dung found periodically on the grave. It seems that they were eating the grass seed before it could take root. Why on this one grave, we do not know, except to say that the topsoil had grown hard and is apparently impenetrable. That is what I imagine when thinking of the path in Jesus' parable.

Jesus' reference to the birds alludes to the devil and his demons. The devil's goal is to deny the hearers of the Word the kingdom-life Jesus offers. The devil's immediate activity is to thwart the Holy Spirit from blessing the ministry of the Word. Specifically, the devil stirs hearers of the Word to so grieve the Spirit by their dishonoring of both the Word he inspired and the sermons he prompts, that the Word becomes of no effect. He and his demons seek in effect to sustain the hearer's spiritual barrenness and the bankruptcy of their hearts and lives.

It is no secret that besides working directly upon the hearer of the Word, the devil uses others around us to accomplish his purposes. He may use the Christian who is naïve to the subtleties of the devil, or the non-Christian oblivious to them. Think of the glee the devil has when we are too busy to spend time with God around his Word, when a family member or friend tries amusing us as the Word is being preached, or when someone suggests switching channels on the radio or television just because a sermon has come on. These are but a few examples of the myriad ways in which the birds come down to snatch away the seed.

I first witnessed this in Wales many years ago. The Lord was really moving at the time. Lori, my future sister-in-law, was converted in those days. The sixth-form common room was becoming abuzz with discussions of Christianity. As a newcomer to personal outreach, I was just learning the ropes, but found that God was granting authority and effectiveness in speaking about Jesus. One girl, Karen, began showing genuine interest in what was going on, even to the point of revealing concern about her eternal destiny. A friend of hers commented: "If you think he's getting to you, just wait until you hear his father!"—a reference to Dad's ministry in the town. I was excited. In my fledgling faith, I must confess that I was amazed she would take interest in the gospel. I never foresaw that someone from the cool crowd would do anything other than ridicule it. After all, doesn't the Bible promise scoffers? Alas, Karen's interest was short-lived. Soon her older sister pressed her not to take things so seriously. Karen took her words to heart. In no time her interest vanished. A fiendish bird had snatched away the seed. Karen's sister was but his mouthpiece. Jesus makes certain we understand the devil's intent: ". . . so that they may not believe and be saved" (Luke 8:12).

CONCLUSION

In actuality, it is highly unlikely that those whose hearts are hardened against God and his Word will have read this chapter. There isn't the spiritual interest to do so. Let us end the chapter, then, with some counsel for those of us whose hearts the Lord has opened. Jesus' reference to the seed landing along the path has relevance to us, too, as it had for the apostles and disciples of his day. The seed landing along the path alerts us to the need to be much in prayer for those yet resisting the Word.

The hearing of sermons intended for the lost is a great opportunity for us to balance our maintenance prayers with frontline praying for the spread of the kingdom. We have a wonderful privilege as citizens of the kingdom to listen to evangelistic sermons prayerfully, storming the gates of the King that he would break up the hardened hearts around us. Only his divine power can bring an end to their trampling of the Word and prevent the devil from snatching away the seed given them. Perhaps the silver lining of the dark and dreadful cloud that has come upon us in the recent voting for the right to full-term abortion is this, that hardened hearts, hidden to the human eye, have been vividly identified by the sight of the clapping and cheering of the passing of legislation affording the freedom to put newborn infants to death. May the sense of repulsion we feel be funneled not only into prayer for them, but for the hardened hearts which would end the lives of these little ones before they get going. We pray not only that they would cease to be complicit in the mass deaths of the pre-born and newly born, but that they would cease to choose for themselves eternal death over eternal life.

The hardened are a great reason for also balancing personal or private prayer with joint, corporate, or communal prayer. The latter is among the foremost expressions of the communion of the saints. Communion or fellowship in prayer is not simply a means of mutual support in our joys and in our sorrows, it is where battles for the kingdom are won:

- Pastors are lionized by the support of God's people. Listen to Paul's urging of the Ephesians to pray "for me, that words may be given to me in opening my mouth boldly to proclaim the mystery of the gospel . . . that I may declare it boldly, as I ought to speak" (Ephesians 6:19-20). Through prayer to God, ministry becomes mighty to the breaking up of hardened hearts.

- Congregants are greatly strengthened to fulfill their vocations with a kingdom mindset. They go back and forth from communal prayer on the wings of the intercession of brothers and sisters for the souls among whom they live and work. They, too, are emboldened to speak the Word of God with authority.

- Above all, God delights to see his people come together, whether as pastors or congregants, to ask him to do what only he can do. Carelessness about God's delight arises either from indifference to the plight of the hardened, from a belief that their hearts are really not that hard, or from a misguided confidence that we have what it takes to soften them or, alternatively, that they are capable of softening themselves. If we cared for the hardened as we should and understood the hardening for what it is, there would be less disappointment in the numbers coming together to storm the gates of heaven.

Some visitors came to our church a number of years back during the week. Guiding them on a tour of the premises, we came to the fellowship hall. Upon entering it, I remarked, "This is where we hold our prayer meeting." I had arranged for it to meet there in the belief that one day it would become normative for the entire church family to be represented in appealing to God to glorify his name through the spread of his kingdom. One of the visitors responded very pointedly, "Do they pray for the ministry of the Word?" I was elated by his question. It was so encouraging. "Now here," I thought, "is a brother who gets the strategic significance of corporate prayer." Corporate prayer does not substitute for private prayer (thereby turning the prayer meeting into a hypocritical façade), but it certainly adds needed dimensions to the prayer life of the church family. The preacher preaches for our equipping, but we come together to pray for his.

If, then, you are of a mind to reinstate or to reinvigorate the prayer meeting in your church, don't neglect frontline prayer. Pray earnestly on the one hand for the Lord to open hearts, and, on the other, to thwart the devil's orchestrated trampling and snatching away of the seed. In the hand of God, such kingdom-oriented prayer serves as a hose through which the water of the Spirit clears the path of traffic. By moistening the path, the Spirit enables the seed to settle in the soil and to grow.

Admittedly, Jesus does not go so far as to envision a future for the seed landing along the path. Neither the context nor the content of the parable leads us to presume that all turns out well for the person whose heart is hardened. Nevertheless, the good soil to which Jesus eventually comes precludes us from writing off the person with the hardened heart. After all, how many of us who now belong to the kingdom of heaven once had hearts like the hardened path? Bearing this in mind, we keep on sowing the seed of the Word. We cannot make it grow, but we trust our sowing of the Word to God. With him all things are possible!

STUDY QUESTIONS: SESSION FOUR

1. Why do you think it is that Jesus' readiness to allow the Word to cut deep into the souls of his hearers is not so emulated or welcome today?

2. What are the chief threats to the primacy and quality of preaching today? How may ministers and congregants unite to underline the importance of both? Share your suggestions.

3. Discuss the respective dangers of preaching aimed lopsidedly at the head and the heart, respectively.

4. What factors do you think make a hearer's heart hard, barren, and exposed?

5. What examples have you observed of the trampling of the seed of God's Word under foot or its snatching away? How may hearers of the Word thwart the devil and the gospel-hardened?

6. How can churches better balance, A. Private and public prayer, and B. Maintenance and frontline prayer? What informs your answers?

Prayer: Dear Lord, we uphold before you those who sow the seed of your Word. May they do so faithfully, in the power of your Spirit, and with the encouragement of your people, so that those whose hearts are hardened may be broken under your Word and rescued by the gospel of your Son, King Jesus. In his holy name we pray. Amen.

In preparation for chapter five, read: Philemon 24, Colossians 4:14, and 2 Timothy 4:10 (about Demas); Hebrews 6:4-6.

5.

THE SEED ON ROCKY GROUND

[5] Other seeds fell on rocky ground, where they did not have much soil, and immediately they sprang up, since they had no depth of soil, [6] but when the sun rose they were scorched. And since they had no root, they withered away.

[20] As for what was sown on rocky ground, this is the one who hears the word and immediately receives it with joy, [21] yet he has no root in himself, but endures for a while, and when tribulation or persecution arises on account of the word, immediately he falls away.

Matthew 13:5-6, 20-21

[5] Other seed fell on rocky ground, where it did not have much soil, and immediately it sprang up, since it had no depth of soil. [6] And when the sun rose, it was scorched, and since it had no root, it withered away.

[16] And these are the ones sown on rocky ground: the ones who, when they hear the word, immediately receive it with joy. [17] And they have no root in themselves, but endure for a while; then, when tribulation or persecution arises on account of the word, immediately they fall away.

Mark 4:5-6, 16-17

[6] And some fell on the rock, and as it grew up, it withered away, because it had no moisture.

[13] And the ones on the rock are those who, when they hear the word, receive it with joy.

But these have no root; they believe for a
while, and in time of testing fall away.

Luke 8:6, 13

Whereas Jesus' description of the seed sown along the path
depicts the absence of a response to the ministry of the Word and
forewarned the crowds before him of the danger of being gospel-
hardened, the seed landing on the rocky ground reveals Jesus'
awareness of the danger of a selective or superficial response.

THE SOWING OF THE SEED

When the sower goes out to sow he knows, whether
consciously or subconsciously, that there are three things he cannot
control, at least not absolutely: where the seed lands, the type of soil
on which it lands, or how the sun will impact the seed that is sown.

The landing of the seed.

The question may already have arisen in your mind, why
does the sower not sow on better soil, or at least do better aiming at
the good soil on his parcel of land. Although he sows by hand and,
therefore, has some control over where the seed lands, the first seed
Jesus mentions landed on the path, and now this seed lands on rocky
ground.

To answer this, we need to recall that parables are illustrative
rather than scientifically precise. More to the point, we recall how
sowing works. The sower doesn't place seeds individually in the
ground. If he did that, he would plant hardly any at all. He scatters
the seed broadly, realizing that even if some seed falls along the path
and some on rocky ground he still has a chance of a better crop than
if he laboriously plants each seed individually. Since that would be a
ridiculously ineffective use of his time, the sower chooses to scatter
the seed far and wide to cover all his land. In fact, he is more
concerned to do that than he is that some seed goes to waste. It is

better, he reasons, that every bit of ground has a chance to produce, even though some seed, landing on poor soil, turns out to be nonproductive. He seeks, then, to scatter wisely, but not in a counterproductive perfectionist sort of way. Even if he went the perfectionist route, he still could not guarantee a corresponding harvest.

The saying I heard during the days of my doctoral research comes to mind: "There are those dissertations which are perfect, and those which are finished!" You get the point. The sower prefers to sow the entire field than to try with his experienced but finite understanding of the soil to sow perfectly but without completing the task or guaranteeing a better crop. After all, he is conscious that the season for sowing passes quickly and that the weather can change abruptly.

The same goes for our present opportunity to proclaim the kingdom. We are in the season of grace, but the faces before us will not always have the opportunity of hearing the Word of the gospel. Some will turn away from the message. Others will be taken away by death. After all, observes British historian Simon Schama, "the scythe of mortality is ever busy, never fussy."[1] Yet others may be here when Christ returns and the sowing of the Word comes to an end. Clearly, time is of the essence. Our sowing must reflect this. The Word of the kingdom is, then, to be proclaimed broadly, generously, and quickly. Our goal is to cover the field in time for there to be a harvest of souls before our season for sowing and our hearers' season for listening runs its course.

There are certain observations preachers can make, such as when, where, and how to sow, but if they start becoming overly selective about the types of hearers to whom the Word is given, then

---

[1] The quotation is taken from memory of Simon Schama's documentary series, *A History of Britain*.

not only will we withhold it from those who may receive it, we will get very little sowing done. We are, then, to be neither laborious nor fastidious in deciding who gets the seed of the Word but are to sow generously and with intent. The apostle Paul understood this very well: "Whoever sows sparingly will also reap sparingly, and whoever sows bountifully will also reap bountifully" (2 Corinthians 9:6).

Christ and the apostles refer to what theologians call the general call of the gospel. Unlike the sower in the parable, however, the distributor of the Word possesses the inexhaustible store of God's Word. He need not, indeed should not, fear he will run out of texts or angles to preach or to share. The Word of God, it is amazing to say, never suffers any depletion when it lands on hearts who refuse it. Writes Paul, "He who supplies the seed to the sower and bread for food will supply and multiply your seed for sowing and increase the harvest of your righteousness" (2 Corinthians 9:10).

Since eternal souls perish when they are not reached with the Word, sowers of the Word have more reason than the sower in the parable for scattering with abandon. We cannot forecast precisely where the seed will grow; therefore, we, too, opt for the saturation approach, waiting upon the Lord to see where the seed will take root. Once the sowing is done, we, like the sower, trust God for the harvest. Whereas the success of our sowing is under God's control, the faithfulness to sow is in ours. We thus scatter the Word liberally, in great hope of a harvest to come.

The type of soil.

The crowd to whom Jesus spoke would have been very familiar with his picture of sowing. They likely knew personally some who sowed the seed each year and were accustomed to seeing them at work. They might not have the experience of the sowers, but all would know the possibility of rocky soil, and that not all rocks can be seen. Note in this regard that Jesus does not say that there was no soil on the rocky ground, but that there was "not much soil" (v. 5). He implies thereby that the rocks lay just below the surface. Low enough to be hidden, but not so low as to afford the seed opportunity to grow strong roots which could grip the soil and grow strong, tall shoots.

How relevant is this scenario to the natural condition of our hearts! When scattering the Word of the kingdom, looks can be deceptive. It can appear that the Word has gone deeper into the hearts of our hearers than the seed which lands on the hardened path (or heart). In the latter scenario, the seed was sown in the heart, but there was no growth whatsoever. In the seed landing on rocky soil there is an immediate response which seems so positive. The seed of the Word reaches the invisible recesses of the heart and from there grows so quickly that it becomes immediately visible.

You may know of those who have shown this sort of growth. Some have gone so far as to publicly profess their faith in the Lord Jesus, having given the impression of a true or life-changing repentance. They shone for a while, offering great encouragement to the leadership and the congregation, raising hopes that a new season of blessing was opening up in the congregation and that other professions of faith would follow.

In a day of small things such as ours, all but the most seasoned of preachers are tempted to forget Jesus' warning of the seed landing on rocky ground. The encouragement is just too good to be spoiled by a dose of realism. The most seasoned, for their part, have to work hard not to allow previous disappointments to breed a self-protective, destructive cynicism which has come to doubt the power of the gospel to transform lives. If spread about unthinkingly, cynicism can harm those in the first flush of their love for the Lord Jesus.

Obviously, then, great pastoral wisdom is needed in weighing professions of faith. The saying of President Ronald Reagan comes to mind: "Trust but verify."

The impact of the sun.

Of the three essentials for the growth of the seed—water, food (the nutrients from the soil), and light—Jesus makes no explicit mention of water (at least in the accounts of Matthew and Mark). The food is common to each of the soils in the parable, although it is practically irrelevant to the seed landing on the path. Ironically, the sun which produces the light necessary for the energy to begin the photosynthesis (the conversion into food) turns out to be counterproductive to the lasting growth of the seed landing on rocky soil. It scorches the shoot since the shoot quickly outgrows its capacity to withstand the Middle Eastern heat.

According to Matthew and Mark, the withering was due to the inability of the germinating seed to put down deep roots in rocky soil. Luke tells us why: it had no moisture (Luke 8:6). In other words, the seed could not recover from the dehydrating impact of the sun since its roots could not reach down beyond the bedrock to the sources of water lurking deeper in the soil. Thus, it shriveled up, disappearing as quickly as it had appeared.

The need, then, for the verification of those professing to be Christ's is real. The author of Hebrews, writing like Matthew to Jews, warns not of their falling from grace, as some have thought, but of the dangers of a temporary inauthentic response to the gospel. It is possible, he says, to have received some sense of general enlightenment about the gospel, to have tasted (rather than eaten) the heavenly gift, to have shared in the Holy Spirit (which is to have felt his influence), and to have tasted (or sampled) the goodness of the Word of God and of the powers of the age to come, only to fall away (Hebrews 6:4-6). This is not a falling away from salvation, but from an adherence to the truth on which salvation is founded. The author of Hebrews has in mind more than a mistaken profession of faith. He rules out restoration to repentance since those he has in mind crucify again the Son of God to their own harm and hold him up to contempt (Hebrews 6:4, 6). He thinks, rather, of those who sprung up to profess faith in Christ, but now no longer own even the truths upon which that profession of faith was based.

The verification needed, given such a possibility, must first be personal. We begin by searching our own hearts. What ought to matter to us and, paradoxically, will if we are genuinely converted, is whether our growth as professing Christians is temporary or permanent. Only a profession of faith which lasts the test of time can be thought of as genuine. Those ministering the Word have, however, the added burden of watching for the type of growth occurring under their spiritual care. Longevity of profession of faith is not the only criterion a spiritual oversight of the Lord's people considers, but longevity does comport with the Lord's promise to keep all those who are his (e.g., 1 Peter 1:5).

THE GROWTH OF THE SEED

The parable of Jesus calls for a humble, cautious, and yet ever hopeful wait-and-see approach to those claiming Christ as their Savior and King. This is perhaps harder to manage emotionally than in the scenario of the seed landing along the path. There the sower would have next to no expectations of a crop and would count it a bonus if anything ever grew on that soil. Likewise, the preacher. Outside of a sovereign intervention by God, he has, left to himself, few if any expectations of the hardest sinner coming to Christ. God is certainly able to save, but the soil is unpromising. In this latest scenario, however, expectations have increased. They need as careful a management by the preacher as by the sower. One way to manage emotions is to consider the growth that becomes visible.

The importance of discerning whether it is temporary or permanent was something I learned early in life. When first professing faith as an eight-year-old, I went on my mother's encouragement to tell my father. I naively thought that he would shoot through the roof with joy. Whether it was because he had just been preaching and was drained, or because he knew me better than I knew myself—I suspect a bit of both—his response was underwhelming to say the least. I can see him now, seated in the vestry of the church, responding with a straight face, "We'll see." As aloof as his response sounds all these years later, his cautious reaction turned out to be justified. Even when, at the age of fifteen, I truly encountered God in Christ, my father's reaction was the same. This was not unbelief on his part, or indifference to the progress of the gospel or to me, for he later relayed to me his conviction from my birth that God would call me into the ministry. Rather, he understood that King Jesus puts more weight by discipleship (permanent growth) than by professions of faith (temporary growth). Accordingly, Dad was more impressed by faith and obedience over the longer haul than by a momentary profession of faith.

This does not mean to say that we should always receive professions of faith in a deadpan sort of way. They are best approached on a case-by-case basis. But there is no doubting the biblical support for putting more value on stable growth than on highly strung claims of conversion, and more on the evidence of submission to Christ than on verbal professions of faith. A person genuinely saved will profess publicly their faith in Jesus Christ, but a verbal profession of faith itself does not guarantee authentic citizenship in the kingdom of heaven.

Consider three telltale signs of a spurious profession of faith.

The growth is sudden.

Although Jesus says in Luke's account that the shoot withers because there was no moisture, we are not to assume that seed had never benefited from moisture. Jesus simply means that at the point at which the seed withered, there was no moisture to hydrate the shoot when the sun was at its hottest.

Although Jesus does not give us all the details, we may assume that there had been some precipitation. After all, both sun and rain are experienced in the Middle East and both were needed for the seed to grow at all.[2] Yet, because of the shallowness of the soil covering the rocky ground, what moisture there had been from dew or rain had gathered, we may presume, in a small pool on the rocks under the surface of the ground. With easy access to these hidden reservoirs the seed quickly grows. To quote Jesus, "It sprang up immediately" (v. 5).

Jesus interprets this phenomenon in terms of the undelayed reception of God's Word (v. 20). It is not just received but received "with joy." This is not the joy that is a fruit of the Spirit (Galatians 5:22), it is the earthly joy the hearer gains from a selective understanding of the Word. He or she has heard what by nature is appealing—the love of God, the forgiveness of sins, and the promise of heaven—but has not weighed the message in an all-around way. He or she focuses on that which is positive but turns a blind eye or deaf ear to the responsibilities of citizenship in Christ's kingdom. Such hearers want entrance into the kingdom of heaven on their own terms rather than on those set by King Jesus. The joy they experience is more of a carnal excitement—"Oh good, look what's coming my way!"—than true blessedness. It differs markedly in quality and quantity from what John Newton (1725–1807) described in his hymn *Glorious Things of Thee are Spoken* as "solid joys and lasting treasures none by Zion's children know."

---

[2] Compare the Psalmist's reference in Psalm 133:3 to the known dew of Mount Hermon further to the north, and to Jesus' reference to rain earlier in Matthew's Gospel (5:45).

Theologians put it this way: By nature we want the benefits of Christ without Christ himself. We want all the King has to offer, but we want neither his fellowship nor his reign over our lives. When we discover that his benefits are spiritual rather than material or temporal, we turn up our noses and walk away. Although in some crass sense such hearers of the Word of the kingdom desire heaven (at least, the evasion of hell), their hearts are set on an easy, self-intoxicated life both here and in the hereafter.

Those truly of the kingdom understand, however, that the perks of our citizenship mean nothing and, in fact, cannot be received without submission to the King. In exclaiming,

> How vast the benefits divine
> Which we in Christ possess!

Augustus Toplady (1740–1778) understood both the vastness of God's saving benefits and their unique location in Christ. They:

- Include our calling, regeneration, and union with Christ.
- Issue in our justification, adoption, and sanctification.
- Are received on the occasion of our faith in Christ and repentance unto God.
- And are treasured through the divine graces of assurance, preservation (or perseverance), and glorification.

In the light of all this, there is no better way to assess sudden growth than by asking a person professing his or her faith what Christ means to them and which benefits of being a Christian they treasure. Those yet remaining in the crowd will falter when faced with such questions. A spiritually discerning eldership will typically be able to tell, either from the content or lifelessness of the answers, whether the sudden growth is temporary. Faced with such a scenario, elders should not be lacking in courage in declining or at least delaying professions of faith. The process of trusting but verifying needs to occur before and not after the door of membership to the church has been opened. Yet, when elders hold shut the doors to membership, they need to be diligent in following up with the applicant with loving pastoral care, with a view to a happier outcome down the road. Such conversations excite for they are wonderful gospel opportunities, but they need to be taken in the right spirit. When such eldership overtures are lost on the false professor, the eldership will at least be at peace that the door of communicant membership was not opened by mistake.

The growth is fragile.

Jesus does not blame the sower for what happens next. He neither says nor hints that the sower should have known better than to sow the seed on rocky ground. Rather, Jesus concentrates on the fact that the seed had no root system capable of sustaining long-term growth. According to his interpretation of the parable, the hearer has "no root in himself" (v. 21). Once more, the problem lies not with the Word of the kingdom, or with the sower, but with the condition of the hearer's heart.

Specifically, the hearer with the stony heart does not take to heart all that is involved in the call to enter the kingdom. He or she has not considered the character of God sufficiently enough, and, therefore, remains under the delusion of thinking that he or she occupies an epicentral standing in God's universe. In this vein, the hearer claims absolute rights over the way he or she lives. What is more, this type of hearer has not come to terms with the gravity of sin—sin's breakage of God's law, rebellion against his holy ways, and its marring of the beauty of his creation.

Having no sense of personal unworthiness, this type of hearer treats Jesus as a means of kicking on in life. Some go to the casino, some to the motivational speaker, some to the financial guru, some to the gym, but this hearer tries out Jesus for size. Jesus makes no suggestion that the sower of the Word has preached erroneously. Rather, the hearer has selectively heard the Word preached, but distorts its message. In his or her mind, the Word is not about the glorification of God in and through his saving purposes in our lives, it is about how Jesus, as an add-on to life, helps us obtain our individual goals.

The last thing such hearers are interested in is personal accountability and conviction of sin. They thus miss out on the "solid joy" of God's grace. Since mercy and forgiveness were never a matter of life or death to them, grace is something they can take or leave. Recall the crowd before Jesus. Most of them were indifferent to their need of saving grace. What they yearned for was the temporal benefit of Christ's next miracle. They failed to see that God's saving grace in Christ *is* the greatest miracle, for it brings us into a relationship *with God* and impacts us *for all eternity*! Appreciating neither this nor the mutual benefit to God and to ourselves of submission to Christ, such hearers are bereft of both gratitude and service to God. With unchanged hearts, they find utterly incomprehensible and not a little distasteful Dietrich Bonhoeffer's observation, that, "When Christ calls a man, he bids him come and die."[3]

Had such hearers given the faithful sower of God's Word a fuller hearing, they would not have sprung up with joy. Had the seed of the Word taken permanent root in them, it would have led them to count the cost of coming under the reign of Christ. Indeed, it is when a person does so, and still wishes to turn to God in repentance, resting in Christ for their acceptance, that we gain confidence that the profession of faith is sincere. In the profession, the emphasis is not on the faith of the responder but on the saving work of Christ. Christ not only saves but supports and sustains through all that

---

[3] Dietrich Bonhoeffer, *The Cost of Discipleship*, Revised and unabridged edition containing material not previously translated (New York: MacMillan Publishing Co., Inc., 1968), 99.

ensues. Growth in him is, then, not fragile, but stubbornly resistant to all that the devil or circumstances throw at us.

The growth is temporary.

Fragile growth is temporary growth. The sun came up and the shoot withered away. Those familiar with the heat-baked Western states of America understand the picture. As one brother reminisced following the preaching of this seed, "You see the same thing in Arizona. The rain pours, and the flowers shoot up! Then the boiling Arizona sun comes up and before you know it the flowers wither away."

How many of us have witnessed hearers of this type vanish as quickly as they appeared! One week they are all engaged in asking questions, attending classes, making friends in the church family, and the next they stop attending; they don't return calls, they dodge believers in the supermarket, and consider their flirtation with Christianity somewhat of an embarrassing fad. Before long they have gone back to their previous life. Christianity was for them but a fleeting episode during an otherwise worldly journey. They understood neither the message, their hearts, nor the blessings and tribulations of the kingdom, but they know very well the world to which they return. They embrace it with renewed zest, accelerating on in life so that their flirtation with Christianity disappears in the rearview mirror as quickly as possible. All the zeal and promises of the moment come to nothing as the coolness they perceive in their religious phase wears off. They leave the Lord's people confused, hurt, and feeling the accusations of the devil that if only they had done more to make "the new convert" feel at home he or she would have hung around.

The parable of the sower reminds us that there will always be those for whom Christianity is but a fad. Their best life, they have decided, is now. With a heavy heart the authentic Christian concurs. Simply put, hearers of this type never belonged to the kingdom. It may have looked briefly as if they had left the crowd behind, but the carnality of the crowd never left them. Jesus, we note, does not depict them as having lost their place in the kingdom (which would be tantamount to their losing their salvation). He indicates, rather, that they never had one. It is all very sad. Indeed, I mourn for those pictured in my mind from whom I learned of this phenomenon. Perhaps you have been mourning likewise as you have read along.

THE WITHERING OF THE SEED

To understand the phenomenon, there are three matters to appreciate.

The occasion of the withering.

In interpreting the parable, Jesus attributes the scorching of the fledgling shoot to the tribulation or the persecution that comes with being his disciples. The tribulations Jesus has in mind are not those of life in general. A person does not have to belong to the kingdom to face trials of sickness, disease, financial heartache, relationship difficulties, and so forth. These are part of life in a fallen world. Jesus was thinking specifically of tribulations belonging uniquely to citizens of the kingdom of heaven. The word translated *tribulation* means *pressure* or *stress* and refers to that which Christians experience on account of their being subject to Christ. Just as the world hated him, so the world hates his disciples.

Since tribulation often precedes persecution, it is no surprise that Jesus mentions them in succession. Tribulation may be described as low-grade persecution: societal bias against the Christian such as discrimination and marginalization. The Christian may be overlooked for social invitations, passed by for job appointments, and ignored by the media.[4] The word used for

---

[4] As I write, Christians the world over are noting how the media has rightly brought to our attention the mass murder of Muslims in Christchurch New Zealand but ignores the thousands of Christians martyred by Muslims in Nigeria

persecution has the idea of pursuit. Accordingly, we may describe tribulation as the world's passive aggression toward the King and those of his kingdom, and persecution as passive aggression ratcheted up to active aggression. The former is idling hostility, the latter is hostility in fuller throttle. It entails the conscious ridiculing of the Christian, the proactive discrediting of him or her through slander and libel, ultimately resulting in physical, emotional, and perhaps fatal harm.

Tribulation and persecution are not to be sought out by the Christian. Nor should they be attributable to our personal offenses or idiosyncrasies. When scandalized by tribulation and persecution we, nevertheless, embrace the experience as citizens of the kingdom. Recalling Jesus' Beatitude helps:

> Blessed are those who are persecuted for righteousness' sake, for theirs is the kingdom of heaven. Blessed are you when others revile you and persecute you and utter all kinds of evil against you falsely on my account. Rejoice and be glad, for your reward is great in heaven, for so they persecuted the prophets who were before you. (Matthew 5:10-12)

We find in tribulation and persecution occasion for pursuing the deeper inner joy of suffering for Jesus. We reason that since he bore for us, through no fault of his own, the ultimate tribulation and persecution, we cannot but rejoice in being associated with him in his suffering (cf., 2 Corinthians 1:5). We glean from him the example of looking to the joy ahead, and thus we despise the present shame (cf., Hebrews 12:2).

---

over the course of recent years. According to the World Watch List, as reported by Open Doors, ninety percent of the 4136 Christians killed for their faith in 2018 were martyred in Nigeria ("Nigeria: 90% of 2018 Christian Deaths Were in Nigeria" by Jacob Ennever [https://www.opendoors.org.au/persecuted-christians/prayer-news/Nigeria-90-of-2018-christian-deaths-were-in-nigeria/, accessed July 25, 2019]).

Church history provides us with some inspirational accounts of true citizens of the kingdom. Consider the example of the early Christian martyr, Vivia Perpetua of Carthage. Imprisoned as a young married woman of twenty-two years of age for professing to be a Christian, her father, an honorable, well-known, and upright citizen of the city, came to the prison to plead with her that she deny her Christianity so as to save her life. He wanted neither personal ruin nor the death of Perpetua and her young son. Perpetua, however, prayed for grace and for her son to know Christ. She had been made a public example by the city authorities, and a wonderful example they got. At her trial she resisted calling herself anything other than what she was, namely, a Christian. On March 7, 203 A.D. she was martyred along with five others, torn apart in the amphitheater by wild beasts, and then finished off by a gladiator's sword. Living in Carthage at the time was a young lawyer, Tertullian, who went on to become the father of Latin theology. To him is attributed the saying, "The blood of the martyrs is the seed of the church."[5]

Tribulation and persecution for the sake of Christ could not distinguish more clearly those belonging to the kingdom from those who do not. The hearers with the hearts like rocky soil quickly fade away when trouble comes. They shrink back without delay into the anonymity of the crowd, if not all the way back into the world. Understandably, then, the early church had real difficulties resolving what to do with those who sought a return to the church once persecution had abated. Were they spurious converts or had they been authentic disciples who fainted in the day of adversity

---

[5] There are numerous accounts of the martyrdom of Perpetua, Felicitas, and three young men, Saturus, Saturninus, and Revocatus. Our depiction is based on Robin Daniel's *This Holy Seed: Faith, Hope, and Love in the Early Churches of North Africa* (Harpenden, Herts: Tamarisk Publications, 1993), 29-38. For a more recent example of joy under persecution, see Sándor Szilágyi's *Sentenced to Joy*, trans. by Péter Pásztor (Kolozsvár: Koinónia, 2019)—an account of Szilágyi's incarceration in Communist-run Romania.

(Proverbs 24:10)? Spurious converts don't tend to return to the church, which is why Jesus' picture of the withering is so final. He had in mind those who, to begin with, were not his.

The cause of the withering.

Significantly, Jesus attributes the withering not to the tribulation or to the persecution in itself but to the Word (v. 21). The problem of the falsely professing Christian is not necessarily that of cowardice. Indeed, the person fading away may in fact be a very courageous person. There may be other issues in life for which he or she would readily suffer tribulation and persecution. What is critical in their fading away from the faith is the fact that it is the Word which scandalizes them. Suffering tribulation and persecution on account of issues in which the world has an interest may make them heroes, but suffering on account of the Word confines their hero status to the church. They are heroes to us because they suffered for Christ and obtained victory through him. Yet, to those held up as heroes and heroines of the faith, Jesus alone is the hero. They know their hearts too well to say otherwise. The hearer with the stony heart is different. He or she is attracted to association with Jesus in his glory, but not in his sufferings. He or she is akin to Perpetua's father who was ashamed to be identified with Christ and his people, hoping against hope that his daughter would not, when faced with death, live up to what she professed to be.

Clearly, then, the hearer of the Word fades away not because Jesus does not solve all his problems, but because he in fact creates some! Not only do hearers of this type not get all they wished for from Jesus, they experience unforeseen pressures of tribulation and persecution which they had not foreseen. Persevering through them is not an option, for such hearers do not have the heart to do so. They have neither the enabling nor the desire to press on. Thus, the preacher's endeavor to comfort them with thoughts of how the Christian's trials are used by God to make us holy and to prepare us for heaven, falls flat. Very flat indeed. This kind of hearer deems likeness to Christ and a heaven as defined by God not worth the trouble. Immediately, says Jesus in effect, they drop the name *Christian*. It did not live up to the ease or the coolness of the life envisioned by a selective reading of Scripture. Hipness and trendiness cannot survive the hostility of the world. In the eyes of the world, Christians will never be either hip or trendy.

In pondering this withering, my mind goes back to days in Sunday School, to the names of persecuted pastors Richard Wurmbrand (1909–2001) and Georgi Vins (1928–1998), and their struggles behind the iron curtain. One particular account remains with me. It haunted me then, and does even now. As I remember it, believers were gathered for worship when in burst two Russian soldiers. They demanded to know which worshipers were Christian, for they were there to shoot them. Anyone not truly Christian could flee the church premises. Some did so, doubtless scurrying shamefaced out of the church building. Once the soldiers were sure all who were going to leave had done so, they locked the door, put their guns down, and explained to the faithful that they, too, were Christian. The draconian measure they had taken was not a prank, but a way of ensuring their own security in participating in the worship. What bonds of fellowship and joy must have followed the withstanding of the test.

Now, allowing for the possibility that some who fled the church were truly the Lord's but "fainted in the day of adversity," the account nevertheless challenges us to the core. What would we do, faced with the same circumstances? Speaking personally, I pray I would remember the words of the apostle Peter, that if anyone suffers as a Christian he must not be ashamed but must rather glorify God (1 Peter 4:16). This is something the hearer with the heart like rocky soil can neither understand nor appreciate. He is simply not up for the enduring of tribulation and persecution for a Jesus he neither loves nor worships, and for divine purposes to which he is indifferent at best.

The result of the withering.

The withering is detected by the shriveling up of the shoot and the death of the seed. Jesus interprets this as "falling away" (v. 21). Again, he is not saying that genuine followers of Christ fall away from grace, but that among those responding to the Word there is a falling away from the company of those belonging to the kingdom. Whether they remain among the crowd claiming some non-costly interest in Jesus or melt into the wider populace of society is a moot point. They reveal in one way or another that they did not belong to the kingdom of heaven. They fall not from salvation but from the hearing of the Word.

Look back over annual church directories, and you will realize that this "falling away" is a live issue. We love to see how, yesteryear, our friends in church once looked and how they dressed. Some hardly change over the years, but others are almost unrecognizable. We skim the rows of photos, turning eagerly from page to page. But then appears the photo which pulls us up short. "Whatever happened to him [or her]?" we ask in all innocence. "Oh, he fell away." Somehow, they were around long enough to get into the pictorial directory, but not long enough to remain present among the members of the kingdom. Former hearers of the Word may still say, if asked their religion on admittance to the hospital or the like, that they are Christian, but they are that in name only. They may cling to some christianese, but they do not cling to Christ nor permit him in love to direct their lives.

CONCLUSION

The seismic cultural shift that has been taking place across the Western world over the last decades is accompanied by an increasing hostility toward Christianity. In business, Sunday opening underlined the preference for materialism and prosperity over spirituality. In education, the opportunities to teach the Bible publicly are challenged if not denied by lobby groups, schools, and councils. In society, the sexual revolution swept aside respect for biblical ethics. In philosophy, feminism insisted that a woman's rights are more valuable than those of unborn males or females killed in their millions.[6] Meanwhile, the LGBTQ movement seeks to squeeze from society the freedom of Christians to disapprove of unbiblical lifestyles.

In such a climate, we can expect and are in fact witnessing two things. First, a fading away of those not up for the tribulation or the persecution. They owned the trappings of Christianity when it was advantageous to do so but are now going AWOL. As a friend who joined a megachurch opined to my wife, "If persecution comes, I doubt 500 of the 5,000 attending would take a stand for Christ." He could, of course, be wrong, but this is a sobering evaluation and quite possibly what Jesus is thinking of when referring to the seed landing on rocky ground.

There is, though, a positive side to what is going on. As we preach the gospel of the kingdom, we can expect fewer false professions of faith. Professing Christ does not appeal to those who see nothing beneficial in an earthly sense to gain from doing so. Such hearers will know from the get-go that if they respond positively to the Word they will be identified as Christian in a context now rightly labeled as Christophobic. We owe it to God and

---

[6] It is said that a staggering 41.9 million unborn babies were killed in 2018 across the world. That is twenty-three percent of all infants conceived and more than the entire populations of 198 out of 233 national populations. How God must be grieved and how the church ought to be. Not self-righteously so, however, since many abortions are, to our shame, requested by those said to be members or affiliates of the professing church. See Thomas D. Williams' blog article "Abortion Leading Cause of Death in 2018 with 41 Million" (https://catholiccitizens.org/uncategorized/82783/abortion-leading-cause-of-death-in-2018-with-41-million-killed/, accessed July 24, 2019).

to hearers of the Word to ensure that there is a counting of the cost of living under the reign of Christ, and that interest expressed in Christ is genuine rather than self-serving. Christ desires not a fickle fan club but lifelong disciples. There is more to walking with Christ than to following a twitter feed! Yet, contrary to the celebrities of our age, he never disappoints.

STUDY QUESTIONS: SESSION FIVE

1. Discuss the factors that are outside of the control of those who sow the seed of the Word. How ought such factors to impact the way it is sown?

2. Why is sowing ultimately a more effective means of the Word than planting? What theological, spiritual, or practical differences underline the two approaches?

3. What criteria may we use to "trust but verify" when there are sudden responses to the Word? Stated alternatively, what came to mind about the telltale signs of the seed on rocky ground?

4. How does the scenario of the seed falling on rocky ground help you process the loss of friends or acquaintances from the Christian community? In your experience, to what degree is the scenario relevant today?

5. The apostle Paul later wrote that, "all who desire to live a godly life in Christ Jesus will be persecuted" (2 Timothy 3:12). In what ways have you faced tribulation or persecution because of the Word?

6. What can members of the kingdom do to encourage themselves in Jesus in a day such as ours in which there is a falling away of those once professing to be Christians?

Prayer: Lord, we praise you for your grace in our lives. Nothing distinguishes us from those whose hearts are as the rocky ground other than your grace! Help us to press on, with "solid joys none but Zion's children know," praying that you would move the hearts of those who persecute and revile your people, so that they would be brought by your love to the feet of King Jesus. Amen.

In preparation for chapter six, read: Genesis 3:1-14.

6

THE SEED AMONG THORNS

[7] Other seeds fell among thorns, and the thorns grew up and choked them.

[22] As for what was sown among thorns, this is the one who hears the word, but the cares of the world and the deceitfulness of riches choke the word, and it proves unfruitful.

Matthew 13:7, 22

[7] Other seed fell among thorns, and the thorns grew up and choked it, and it yielded no grain.

[18] And others are the ones sown among thorns. They are those who hear the word, [19] but the cares of the world and the deceitfulness of riches and the desires for other things enter in and choke the word, and it proves unfruitful.

Mark 4:7, 18-19

[7] And some fell among thorns, and the thorns grew up with it and choked it.

[14] And as for what fell among the thorns, they are those who hear, but as they go on their way they are choked by the cares and riches and pleasures of life, and their fruit does not mature.

Luke 8: 7, 14

It is possible that neither of the responses to date depicts us or those we know. In the one response, there is no movement toward God; in the other a response that is rapid but fleeting. There is, however, a third response. It seems to fall between the tempo of the first two. The seed which fell among the thorns grows up (unlike the seed on the path), but it does not "spring up" as does the seed which fell on rocky ground.

UNDERSTAND THE THORNS

Jesus, as Son of God and agent in creation, would have been more conscious than any of the crowd before him of the significance of thorns. Although the Old Testament tells us that God beheld his creation and pronounced it "very good," the thorns in their sharpness and challenge to the cultivation of the earth arose as a result of the subsequent fall of man. Recall God's judgment on our first parents. To Adam he said:

> Because you have listened to the voice of your wife and have eaten of the tree of which I commanded you, "You shall not eat of it," cursed is the ground because of you; in pain you shall eat of it all the days of your life; thorns and thistles it shall bring forth for you; and you shall eat the plants of the field. By the sweat of your face you shall eat bread, till you return to the ground, for out of it you were taken; for you are dust, and to dust you shall return (Genesis 3:17-19).

The Fall casts, then, a shadow across the parable. The shadow is clear in each scenario of the rejection of the Word, but the thorns make it especially clear. Three observations may be made of them.

The thorns are already in the ground.

Thorns are somewhat mysterious. We don't see anyone scattering thorn seeds, nor do we read of that happening. Yet, they protrude from the soil, seemingly without origin or end. Evidently, they have no problem gripping the soil, and likely have grown thick and strong since no one is in a hurry to deal with them. They neither yield produce nor flowers, and yet they do not struggle for growth. Rather, they hinder the growth of the seed which does produce.

This is as it is with our hearts! No one sows the thorn seed. We inherit it from our fallen parents and call it original sin. By nature, our hearts yield neither produce nor flowers of righteousness, but they bring forth naturally and inevitably the thorns of actual sin. Just as the thorns indicate the condition of the soil, so our sins speak volumes of the state of our hearts. It would be better if the soil produced nothing than to produce thorns, for not only are the thorns worthless and warrant being cut down and burned in a fire, they hinder good growth.

The thorns occupy the space.

The thorns with their deep roots grow thick and strong and occupy space in the ground. Even when the seed falls in the vicinity of the thorns and manages to take root, the seed is unable to grow sufficiently to find the strength to push aside the thorns and to emerge from their shadow.

The spiritual application is obvious enough. While we cannot get the Word of the kingdom out to hearers prior to their possession of original sin, we must get it out to children and to young people before the thorns of actual sin grow deep, thick, and strong in their hearts. Since these thorns grow naturally and wildly, there is no time for delay. It does not take long for corrupt natures to become manifest in strong and abiding patterns of sin. These complicate markedly the chances of the seed finding the space and the light needed to take root and to grow.

The primary onus for the sowing of the seed in the hearts of children lies with parents. Parenthood is a wonderful privilege, but how weighty is the spiritual responsibility involved in the care of children. Later in Matthew's Gospel, Jesus went so far as to say that if anyone causes little children to sin, it would be better for him (or for her) to have a heavy millstone (used for grinding grain) fastened around his neck and to be cast into the depth of the sea (18:6). Jesus is obviously speaking figuratively. He says in effect that an inevitable drowning is better, in itself, than facing the wrath of God for leading little ones into ways of sin.

This is how seriously Jesus takes the spiritual care of children. He came to conquer sin with its attending misery of guilt and corruption, enslavement and destruction. When we understand this theologically and feel personally even the temporal consequences of our own sins, we receive a burden to do all in our power to protect young children from sin. We cannot of ourselves root out the thorn of original sin, but we are in earnest to limit the opportunities for actual sin to grow. There is no better way to do that than by introducing them as early as possible to the majestic power of Christ. He not only forgives, he liberates from sin. I am not, then, encouraging parents to be heavy-handed or legalistic, for such strictures are counterproductive. They only end up encouraging sin. I am, however, urging us to preach the evil and destructive consequences of sin and, vitally so, the gracious and liberating power of Christ.[1]

This passion to safeguard children from sin arises from observing how young people sleep-walk into its heartache and ruin. We know from personal experience that the young can be vulnerable to the lies of Satan, to peer pressure, and to the heart's deception and rebellion. Faithful parents will warn their children that sin does not pay, but children are not always disposed to listen to their parents.

---

[1] We need to be clear in our minds and in our motivation, however, that what we denounce to children as sin (or at least as a wisdom issue) is not a mere cultural more that we heighten to the category of divine law-breaking (or folly) simply because we find it distasteful. Such restrictions on the liberties of the young, supposing they succeed (often they provoke a reaction opposite to the one desired), breed an atmosphere of fear, avoid critical heart issues, and create many pastoral issues which later come to the surface. Many is the middle-aged person who traces his or her rejection of Christianity back to an upbringing in a Christian home where parents, while earnest, went beyond Scripture in their censures, or where scriptural censures were applied unlovingly.

Sometimes parents are faithful but are afraid of holding the difficult conversations. Other parents are not faithful but foolish and beget and conceive children before they are spiritually positioned to warn their young ones of the devastation caused by sin. Oftentimes, and the more so as society abandons the notion of moral absolutes, parents (frequently single parents) are still busy working through (or not as the case may be) the fallout from their own sleepwalking into sin. Thus, the enslavement and disfunction becomes a cross-generational pattern.

It was with an aching heart, that I felt, as a pastor, compelled on one occasion to read to a congregant Jesus' warning about the millstone (Matthew 18:6). I feared doing so, seeking neither the wrath of the mother (the father was not on the scene) nor the upset of the family (although the grandmother who was present understood my intent and shared my concern). To be clear, I didn't read the passage simply because her newborn was illegitimate. I did so, fearing for the child in entering her mother's world, but also in prayerful hope that the Lord would use the reading to awaken the mother. "What good would it do this child," I pondered, "if, having been cooed over through her early years of cuteness, she is led thereafter into psychologically destructive, emotionally enslaving, and spiritually damnable paths of sin?"

To some, my choice of reading likely missed the memo about a maternity ward being a place of celebration. Yet, to be pro-life in the fullest sense is to care for a child's soul as well as his or her body. Christianese focuses on the care of the body, but it takes the indwelling of Christ in our hearts for our care of infants and young children to extend to their souls. This care Jesus had in mind when making his shocking pronouncement.

Undoubtedly, parents need the help of the church in rearing their young. Preachers, elders, Sunday School teachers, and youth leaders not only instruct parents and their children in the Word of

God, they also influence how the children are to be taught. The teaching of the children occurs, then, in what can be a very productive partnership between the nuclear family and the church family. As parents rely on churches for faithful support in nurturing their children, so the church looks to parents to actively fulfill their calling (and vows where the child has been baptized) in sowing at home the seed of the Word. Rightly do parents voice their concerns when the church lets down their children; but pastors, elders, Sunday School teachers, and youth leaders understandably become deflated and grieved, when, for all the work of the church in catering to the spiritual needs of the young, parents are negligent about the means of grace on the Lord's Day and the modeling of spiritual priorities for their children during the week. Both Holy Scripture and experience teach us that today's neglected child is, apart from God's intervention, tomorrow's unbelieving, enslaved, dysfunctional, and lost adult.

The thorns grow up and choke the seed.

Even when the seed lands on the thorny soil and actually puts down roots, there is no guarantee of it producing fruit. The thorn-laden overgrowth blocks the sunlight and the rain which the seed needs for its growth. Under such conditions the seed dies. Again, the problem lies not with the seed but with the conditions. The hearer allows his heart to become so cluttered by the wild thorns of sin that the seed sown in the heart has very little chance to grow and to prosper. Thus, we urge parents to put themselves and their children under the preached Word as early and as often as they can, both at home and by consistent weekly attendance at church. This is especially needed, now that access to Bibles in public schools is increasingly limited. As a widely available instagram caption remarks (replete with pictures), "Bibles aren't allowed in schools anymore but are encouraged in prison. If kids were allowed to read it at school, they may not end up in prison."

If you are a parent I implore you to do all in your power to clear the calendar to ensure your family is present for regular family worship and in public worship each Lord's Day. If, as a parent, you are yet outside of Christ's kingdom, you need not wait until entering it to reorder your priorities. The reordering does not take priority over your need to enter the kingdom, nor can the reordering gain you admission to Christ's kingdom. Nevertheless, it signals your intent to seek God and to influence your family in doing so. If, conversely, you already profess citizenship of the kingdom of heaven, and are living your life under the reign of Christ, take heart. It is by the Word that God puts an axe to the root of your thorns and can help you to speak with biblical and spiritual authority to your children.

Indeed, it is by investing spiritually in ourselves that we invest likewise in our children. One investment tool we call the mortification (or putting to death) of sin. The more we mortify it, the more we create the space and let in the light needed for the seed of the Word to grow in our hearts. To quote Jesus' later parable in the sequence, the parable of the seed growing, "first the blade, then the ear, then the full grain in the ear" (cf., Mark 4:28). The more, in turn, our children see our growth, the less excuse they have for allowing the thorns of sin to grow in their own hearts.

Children will never have perfect parents, but how many have been influenced for good by a dad or a mom, preferably both, who held God in reverential awe, who took seriously the claims of Christ over their lives, and who pursued his purposes in life. Countless numbers in eternity will testify as to how they were led to Christ by the lips and lives of their parents, and will perceive how, under the good hand of God, they were spared the heartaches of sin by the evident disdain their parents had for it. Sometimes, that disdain was very costly. In American culture where, to cite the well-known outspokenness of Prince Philip, parents obey their children so well, spare a thought for those fathers and mothers who "seek first the kingdom" (Matthew 6:33) and thus, in pursuing the longer term spiritual health of their children, have to ride out storms of abuse from rebellious children. They sacrifice a false peace in prayerful hope of the appearance of God's glory in the family through the salvation, holiness, and usefulness of their children in time to come. That is how spiritual dynasties are established.

IDENTIFY THE THORNS

The thorns are varied. Jesus has especially in mind the cares of the world, the deceitfulness of riches, and the desire for other things/pleasures. Interestingly, he does not say that cares, riches, and pleasures are sinful in themselves. After all, cares are part of the insecurities of life in a fallen world, financial resources are necessary, and desires and pleasures are gifts from God. Yet, as fallen creatures, we turn that which is innocent or neutral into occasions of sin.

The cares of the world.

The cares Jesus has in view are those which divide the mind. Our bodies sit before the preacher, the hearer digests the words heard, but the focus of the mind lies elsewhere. The hearer not only has different interests from those around him in worship, his interests, says Jesus, are anxious. This hearer is not anxious about his sin and the importance of being forgiven and of coming under the transformative reign of Christ. Rather, his anxious interests are "of the world." His internal life is preoccupied with, literally, the cares "of the age" (v. 22). All the while the preacher urges him to shun hell and to gain heaven he is taken up with the limited horizons and worldly concerns of this life.

Listen to my brother, Andy, and his testimony of his experience in worship before coming to Christ. He left home for the British forces' junior army at the age of sixteen and left the regular army nine years later. Out of respect for our parents with whom he was living once back on "civvy street," he returned to attending church. He recalled how those observing him in worship remarked how well he listened to the sermons given that he had made no profession of faith. "I wasn't listening at all. I was used to standing to attention on the parade ground for ages and found no problem in sitting to attention during church services. I may have looked as if I was listening intently, but my mind was elsewhere." In other words, the thorns of this world's cares were wrapped around his mind and heart. Bodily he was present, but spiritually he was in a very different place.

Cares become sinful when they are untimely, when they concern illegitimate matters, or legitimate ones processed without trust in God and in a way preventing us from hearing from God or from following through on his invitations and directives. Perhaps you know such cares very well. You have every access to God's Word, and are found in hearing distance of it, either periodically (Christmas, Easter, funerals, and weddings) or regularly (on the Lord's Day), but your cares lie elsewhere. There is no concern in this life, however, which has a right to overshadow or to nullify the care we should have to enter the kingdom. Heed the lyrics of Helen Lemmel. They remain as true today as when she penned them in 1922:

> Turn your eyes upon Jesus,
> Look full in this wonderful face,
> And the things of earth will grow strangely dim,
> In the light of his glory and grace.

The deceitfulness of riches.

Jesus doesn't say, nor does the Bible at large, that riches in themselves keep us from hearing the Word of God. They only facilitate neglect of the Word when we love them to the point of idolatry, when we sin in acquiring them, when they hold us back from taking on board what God is saying to us in his Word, or when we are deceived by them into thinking they count for more than they do. If we believe this life to be defined by riches and that those we collect impact our destiny or standing in the next, then, exclaims Jesus in effect, "You are deluded!" For sure, we ought to be good stewards of our finances, but no matter the size of our bank balances, God and his Word are the most precious blessings a person can have. As the saying goes, "there are no pockets in a coffin."

The desire for other things/pleasures of life.

Mark and Luke add a third thorn inhabiting the heart: "the desire for other things" (Mark 4:19) or the "pleasures of life" (Luke 8:14). They are like an "etc." at the end of the list. They become sinful when they substitute for desires for God and the pleasures found in him. By that point they have become idols. No person clinging self-consciously to them can cross over into the kingdom, any more than a person carrying forbidden goods can receive a pass from a border control agent to enter another country. Certainly, our understanding of the gravity of idolatry matures once we are living under the reign of Christ, but no one is granted entrance into the kingdom of heaven who seeks to bring their idols with them.

The relevant desires or pleasures of life vary from person to person. Think of those thorns in your life which occupy your mind and heart when you hear the Word but choke its effect. Are you, for example, a person forever seeking popularity but deaf to Jesus' warning, "Woe to you when all men speak well of you" (Luke 6:26)? Or, perhaps you want a standing with Jesus in the next life, but you cannot bring yourself to risk losing, on account of Christ, your standing in this one. Unlike the person with the heart like rocky ground, you actually count the cost of entering the kingdom, but you calculate the cost to be too high. Your social pursuits, for instance, are too valuable to forgo for the sake of spreading Christ's kingdom. In which case, you are deaf to Jesus' claim that he came to dispense life (as opposed to mere existence), and that those possessing it in him may have it abundantly both here and in the life to come (John 10:10).

Rather, Satan, who we are told in the same text in John's Gospel, "comes to kill, steal, and destroy," has successfully duped you into thinking that Christ's offer to reign over your life is foreboding and life inhibiting. He has got you thinking that Christ is a killjoy. Thus, you hold on to the sins in your pleasures and desires of life which war against your soul instead of submitting to Jesus' life-giving reign over your soul. You cling, for example, to your unconverted boyfriend or girlfriend thinking you will be happier than you could be in Christ, or you remain outside the kingdom just in case your spouse does not care for the new you that inevitably will emerge under Christ's sovereign refashioning of your desires, company, and purpose in life. It is true, your spouse may indeed despise your love of Christ and of his will for your life. But it is also possible that he or she may be drawn to Christ by his gracious transforming of your life. After all, your spouse may not be too taken with the current you! Regardless, you will never know how he or she reacts unless or until you recognize that you need Christ in your life more than the unreliable securities in which you trust.

When you come to rest in Christ, you will discover that since he is able to forge for you an entrance into his kingdom, he is able also to take care of your "other things" and the "pleasures of life." After all, King Jesus is never in debt to anyone. As faithful members of the kingdom attest, he becomes our all-surpassing satisfaction. This explains how John Paton, having left the comparative comfort of Scotland for a life as a pioneer missionary on the New Hebrides, could exclaim: "Oh that the pleasure-seeking men and women of the world could only taste and feel the real joy of those who know and love the true God—a heritage which the world and all that pertains thereto cannot give to them, but which the poorest and humblest followers of Jesus inherit and enjoy!"[2] Such satisfaction only follows the decision to rest in Christ. It does not precede it. We take the Lord Jesus at his word or not at all.

CONFESS THE THORNS!

Thorns are there to be hacked away at, to be taken away, and to be burned. They are an evidence of the Fall and serve no good purpose. Yet, we tend to leave them unless or until we see them as a problem or as an eyesore.

I live in a quiet and friendly community. It is a residential area where moms walk and run alone, where the elderly stroll the streets exercising their dogs, and where neighbors stop to chat. In the winters, we dutifully tidy our drives by snowblowing them or by hiring snowplowers. In the spring and the summer, we make sure our yards are mowed and our flowers are blooming. Yet, in the time I have lived in the neighborhood, there has been one house on the adjacent street that has been different. There was no driveway for it was entirely overgrown. The thorns and briers smothered the mailbox, a tree grew wildly in the front yard. It was difficult to see the house behind all the brush. It looked as though nobody lived there. Surely the eyesore devalued the homes on either side of it. New owners, however, have now taken control of the situation. All the wild brush has been cut away and taken away, the house is now visible and has been cleaned up. The mailbox is now visible, fresh landscaping has been completed, and a new driveway has been laid. If you were a newcomer to the street you would never guess how the house looked previously.

Whether the former owners could see what was obvious enough to everyone else is unknown. The situation was disastrous.

---

[2] *John G. Paton: Missionary to the New Hebrides*, first published 1889; reprint ed. (Edinburgh and Carlisle, PA: The Banner of Truth Trust, 1994), 78.

So is the natural state of our hearts. The heart allows the unlovely and unproductive thorns of sin to grow wild, and the more they do so the more we realize our inability to control them or to root them out. The situation has no hope of improvement unless there is first a recognition of how bad it is. Not only are our hearts unsightly on account of the reign of indwelling sin, they also prevent fruit-yielding seed from prospering, and thus they remain unfruitful.

Jesus' understanding of unfruitfulness.

At the heart of personal unfruitfulness is the rejection of the Word of God. Whereas God has intended his Word to be our rule of faith and conduct—how we may know him and glorify him by our lives—our penchant for the cares of the world, the deceitfulness of riches, and the desire for other things/pleasures in life, clearly indicates that an alternative (that is, nonbiblical) philosophy and style of life is in operation, one which omits thought of God and of his glory.

The *cares of the world* are unfruitful because they do not encourage or instill trust in God. Recall how Jesus spoke of these earlier in Matthew's Gospel, in the Sermon on the Mount:

> Which of you by being anxious can add a single hour to his span of life? And why are you anxious about clothing? Consider the lilies of the field, how they grow: they neither toil nor spin, yet I tell you, even Solomon in all his glory was not arrayed like one of these. But if God so clothes the grass of the field, which today is alive and tomorrow is thrown into the oven, will he not much more clothe you, O you of little faith? Therefore do not be anxious, saying, "What shall we eat?" or "What shall we drink?" or "What shall we wear?" For the Gentiles seek after all these things, and your heavenly Father knows that you need them all. But seek first the kingdom of God and his righteousness, and all these things will be added to you (Matthew 6:27-33).

Anxiety over the cares of this life are futile for they neither bring us closer to God nor do they change our earthly circumstances. That is why Jesus urges his hearers to prioritize the seeking of the kingdom. In possessing Christ, citizens of the kingdom have the assurance that all earthly cares are in the best of hands.

Riches are unfruitful because they lead a person to invest their all solely in this life. Life is slipping through our fingers moment by moment. Said the wise woman of Tekoa, "We must all die; we are like water spilled on the ground, which cannot be gathered up again" (2 Samuel 14:14). With the last drop of life, our acquired wealth is gone. The Egyptians thought otherwise and stacked the pyramids with treasures they believed the pharaohs would need in the afterlife. Archaeology has proven otherwise. The treasures discovered lay exactly where they were placed thousands of years ago. If, by contrast, our riches are spiritual, they are being stored up in heaven as the unending, uncorrupted, and uncorrupting reward for those living their lives in gratitude to God and in joyful submission to the reign of Christ.

The *desire for other things or for the pleasures of this life* are unfruitful because they so often prove counterproductive to our welfare. The philosopher Epicurus (341–271 B.C.) had some understanding of this. He taught that the goal of life is happiness (the absence of pain and mental disturbance). Epicurus defined happiness by coupling what he regarded as two infallible criteria: sensations and perceptions of pleasure. Many may never have heard of Epicurus, but they live out of his philosophy of life, perhaps with one important exception. Unlike Epicurus they forget that, if we are to avoid pain and havoc, pleasure must be pursued short of its diminishing returns. They seek highs from dangerous adventure but experience injury or death, from drug-use but daily battle its life-ruining affects, and from instant sexual gratification but are now shamed and embarrassed by STDs. The list could go on. Not only can today's Epicureans not control the fallout from their philosophy of life (since they cannot always tell the exact point at which pleasure turns to pain), the pleasures upon which they fixate are not the highest nor the holiest which God has for us. C. S. Lewis' oft-repeated observation comes to mind:

> If we consider the unblushing promises of reward and the staggering nature of the rewards promised in the Gospels, it would seem that Our Lord finds our desire not too strong, but too weak. We are half-hearted creatures, fooling about with drink and sex and ambition when infinite joy is offered us, we are like ignorant children who want to continue making mud pies in a slum because we cannot imagine what is meant by the offer of a vacation at the sea. We are far too easily pleased.[3]

That easy but fading pleasures are what Jesus drives at when thinking of the unfruitfulness of those who prioritize them ahead of the kingdom we are to seek first.

Jesus' concern with unfruitfulness.

Jesus says that those lives not bearing spiritual fruit receive judgment. The judgment begins in this life where there is continual impenitence, resulting, as we have seen, in a closing down of opportunities to repent. But this preliminary judgment is confirmed and activated in the life to come. Jesus had already made this point in his earlier use of the agricultural theme: "Every tree that does not bear good fruit is cut down and thrown into the fire" (7:19). Jesus was not relishing such a prospect, for unfruitful lives deny his Father the honor due him and fail to fulfill their divinely ordained purpose. Nevertheless, if we are not bringing forth good fruit—that is, good attitudes and works arising from submission to King Jesus and offered to God for the display of his glory—then we are bringing forth bad fruit. Bad fruit includes not only sinful attitudes and works of the flesh, but apparently good attitudes and works exhibited other

---

[3] C. S. Lewis, "The Weight of Glory" in *The Weight of Glory and Other Addresses*, Ed. W. Hooper (New York, Simon and Schuster, 1996), 25-26.

than in Christ's name and for the glory of someone other than God. Typically, ourselves!

The apostle Paul was later to underline Christ's warning:

> Do you not know that the unrighteous will not inherit the kingdom of God? Do not be deceived: neither the sexually immoral, nor idolaters, nor adulterers, nor men who practice homosexuality, nor thieves, nor the greedy, nor drunkards, nor revilers, nor swindlers will inherit the kingdom of God.

He was writing to those in the morally anarchic city of Corinth, stating in effect that the cultivation of the thorns of the heart is no evidence of the receipt of Christ nor of his gracious gift of citizenship in his kingdom. To the Christian, this is obvious enough, and, yet, living in days where some of the sins Paul lists are now defended as personal rights and others as mistakes or illnesses, we can only lament the level of deception abroad today. Deception not only misleads, it plays down the necessity and clarity of the gospel. No such confusion existed in Paul's mind, nor, it seems, in the minds of the Corinthian believers. Paul continues: "And such were some of you. But you were washed, you were sanctified, you were justified in the name of the Lord Jesus Christ and by the Spirit of our God" (1 Corinthians 6:9-11). Paul refers to the way God had set apart the Corinthian believers from the world about them. He refers to what we nowadays call *definitive sanctification*. By the label we refer to the believer's once-for-all separation from the world unto God. Without it there can be no progressive sanctification (growth in grace) nor final sanctification (perfection in holiness).

CONCLUSION

What does all this say to us? If the seed sown by the ministry of the Word in our lives is nonproducing, then the time has come to ask ourselves whether we remain in the crowd. It is possible to possess a conservative or traditional view of the social issues of the day and yet to remain a cultural "Christian." That is what we are if we are content to leave alone the thorns of sin in our hearts. This is not what God intends for his people, nor what Christ intends in reigning over us as his subjects. When, then, the thorns continue to grow and to choke the seed of the Word, we need to ask ourselves whether we have entered the kingdom of heaven and are submitting to the will of Christ the King. His power, operative in the Christian by the Holy Spirit, breaks down the thorns, enabling us to clear them gradually from our hearts over the course of our lives.

There's more to Christianity, then, than an intellectual fascination with Jesus. Certainly, a person entering the kingdom retains that. In fact, it is a major red flag for a professing believer not to be taken up with Christ. This fascination ought to grow the more we know him. As the years unfold, our knowledge of Christ becomes broader, deeper, and higher. Yet, to the fascination of the mind God adds emotional and volitional elements. Our affections become suffused with Christ, while our wills seek increasingly to conform to his. Paul, meditating much on the kingdom of God, summed up this fascination with Christ when writing to the Colossians, that "Christ is all, and in all" (Colossians 3:11). He was not comparing him to the Father and the Spirit, thereby declaring himself to be a Christomonist (regarding Christ as sole representative of the Trinity). Rather, he was comparing Christ to what this world has to offer.

How contrary is the content and feel of today's christianese. In the United States, cultural "Christians" profess Christ but place the American dream front and center. Observes David Platt,

> self reigns as king (or queen), we have a dangerous tendency to misunderstand, minimize, and even manipulate the gospel in order to accommodate our assumptions and desires. As a result we desperately need to explore how much of our understanding of the gospel is American and how much is biblical. And in the process we need to examine whether we have misconstrued a

proper response to the gospel and maybe even missed the
primary reward of the gospel, which is God himself.[4]

Hence our study. We are asking whether our Christianity is taken up
with Christ the King, or with a dream in which a superficial
"christianese" disguises our intent to reign supreme.

If you find yourself depicted by the seed landing among
thorns, then I encourage you to get alone with God, to quietly reflect
in his presence. Humbly ask him to show you three things:

- *The thorns in your hearts.* They neither please God nor offer
  satisfaction. Rather, they reveal the futility of life outside the
  kingdom.

- *The power of the King.* At the cross Christ destroyed the
  works of the devil and by his Spirit Christ illuminates
  darkened minds, subdues rebellious hearts, and redirects
  stubborn wills.

- *The need you have of repentance toward God and faith in the
  Lord Jesus Christ.* These are both gifts of God's grace
  without which we cannot enter the kingdom of heaven.

As you pray, presume nothing, yet take heart. It is God's revealed
will that the seed of his Word bears fruit unto his glory. He has
promised to answer affirmatively all who diligently seek him (cf.,
Acts 2:21; Hebrews 11:6).

While we do not receive God's grace for surrendering to
Christ (as if grace were a reward), we receive no saving grace
without such a surrender. If, then, you come away from your time of
reflection, thankful that by God's grace you have entered the

---

[4] David Platt, *Radical: Taking Back Your Faith from the American Dream*
(Colorado Springs, CO: Multnomah Books, 2010), 28.

kingdom, then in love be fully in, surrendering more and more to Christ in ever widening and deepening areas of your life.

Naturally, so long as there is remaining sin in us there will always be room for greater surrender. However, to claim to be of the kingdom without being at all surrendered to Christ is as impossible as it is to be the so-called *carnal Christian.* An unsurrendered citizen of Christ's kingdom is as unheard of in Scripture as a Christian desiring, habitually, the works of the flesh over the fruit of the Spirit. To quote from a social media feed citing Francis Chan's *Crazy Love*: "Lukewarm living and claiming Christ's name simultaneously is utterly disgusting to God." The spirit of the genuine citizen of the kingdom is summarized, rather, by Judson W. VanDeVenter's hymn of 1896 (altered 1890):

> All to Jesus I surrender, all to him I freely give;
> May I ever love and trust him, in his presence daily live.
>
> All to Jesus I surrender, humbly at his feet I bow,
> worldly pleasures all forsaken, take me Jesus take me now.[5]
>
> All to Jesus I surrender, make me Savior, wholly thine;
> may thy Holy Spirit fill me, may I know thy power divine.
>
> All to Jesus I surrender, Lord, I give myself to thee;
> fill me with thy love and power, let thy blessing fall on me.

No matter, then, the remaining areas in our lives of needed self-surrender to Christ, authentic citizens of the kingdom resonate, when walking in the Spirit, with VanDeVenter's aspiration to be fully

---

[5] I cannot vouch for the intention of VanDeVenter here, but believe that the surrender of worldly pleasures to Jesus requires not a banning of all pastimes, but of those which are outrightly sinful, or which threaten through the idolatrous pursuit of them to subjugate the claims of Christ over our lives. I am not advocating then a narrow pietistic asceticism but a richer piety which enjoys God's world in ways pleasing to him and which practices his presence amid that enjoyment.

surrendered. Our attitude to Christ helps, accordingly, to reveal where we stand, whether inside the kingdom or outside of it, and, if in, whether we are fully in or not.

STUDY QUESTIONS: SESSION SIX

1. How does the picture of the thorns illustrate the history and reality of original sin?

2. Since we cannot get the Word of the kingdom to children before the presence of original sin in their lives, discuss the importance and process of getting it to them before their corrupt natures manifest strong, engrained, and abiding patterns of actual sin.

3. Discuss how the sowing of the seed among the young is goingin your family and in your church. Stay clear of destructive criticism, focusing on how the sowing and the receiving can be encouraged.

4. What is it about the thorns Jesus mentions (and any which come to your mind) which choke the seed of the Word? Share ways you see that happening today.

5. How does Jesus' view of a fruitful life differ from society's subliminally or explicitly stated view?

6. What deceptions of sin and its judgment do you perceive today, and how may we counter such deceptions? Discuss.

Prayer: O Lord God, forgive us for rendering your Word ineffective by our sins and for reaping thereby judgment on ourselves in this life and in the life to come. Rid our lives, we pray, of the thorns which have choked the seed of your Word and grant us the grace to surrender to Christ more and more. For your glory's sake we pray these things. Amen.

In preparation for chapter seven, read: Galatians 5:1-26

7

THE SEED ON GOOD SOIL

[8] Other seeds fell on good soil and produced grain, some a hundredfold, some sixty, some thirty.

[23] As for what was sown on good soil, this is the one who hears the word and understands it. He indeed bears fruit and yields, in one case a hundredfold, in another sixty, and in another thirty."

Matthew 13:8, 23

[8] And other seeds fell into good soil and produced grain, growing up and increasing and yielding thirtyfold and sixtyfold and a hundredfold."

[20] But those that were sown on the good soil are the ones who hear the word and accept it and bear fruit, thirtyfold and sixtyfold and a hundredfold."

Mark 4: 8, 20

[8] And some fell into good soil and grew and yielded a hundredfold."

[15] As for that in the good soil, they are those who, hearing the word, hold it fast in an honest and good heart, and bear fruit with patience.

Luke 8:8a, 15

By now you are likely thinking, "Does *anybody* receive the seed of God's Word?" The layout of the parable might lead us to this thought, but for many discouraged preachers this is the question which weekly haunts them. They spend their lives laboring in Word and doctrine but see little fruit for their endeavors. They stress prayer for the gospel alongside prayer for the congregation's personal needs and, at their best, to enact faithful and effective congregational outreach. Yet, they face the temptation to throw in the towel since, for all their efforts, they observe unconverted attendees becoming gospel-hardened and see little response to their endeavors to interact with the surrounding community.

Discouragement, we repeat from earlier, is not a very reliable witness to what God is doing, for it exaggerates the negative. Professing members in the congregation are, by contrast, living testimonies to the fact that there are always those who receive the Word. Today, many churches are emptier in North America than they were thirty years ago, and in Europe many are being sold off or pulled down. But look how the kingdom of heaven has spread phenomenally on the Korean peninsula over the last century. It is said that more Christians are coming to faith in Iran today than over the last 1,300 years! Mission India puts out a color-coded map of the subcontinent which, in a very few years, has changed color due to the numbers coming to faith there. Listen to the report of John DeVries, erstwhile President of Mission India:

> Our Indian partners (some 1,500 Indian missions) reach one and a half million persons with the gospel each year and see them become new believers as a direct result of the Spirit's working through one of our three training programs.

> Twenty-five hundred church planters are being trained annually, five million boys and girls are being impacted through our two-week Bible Clubs every summer, and nearly 500,000 illiterate people have become literate and have started businesses that increase their income by an average of 55%. That isn't even the greatest result. These Indian missions are starting about 10,000 new churches per year, and each of those is reproducing new churches. These churches are bringing the good news to the

largest unreached nation on earth, a place where one out of every six people in the world lives.[1]

We may pose questions about the theological oversight and orthodoxy of such church plants and the lengths to which Mission India and her partners go in measuring the crop, but who can deny that God is on the move in the subcontinent. For all that, 2018 was the first year on record that Africa was said to have more Christians than any other continent—an admittedly broadly defined 631 million or forty-five percent of the population of the African population.[2] The number of professing Christians in the world has nearly quadrupled since 1910, although the number has not kept pace with the phenomenal growth of the world's population to over 7 billion.[3]

The bottom line is this: Christ has promised that his kingdom will never fail, and we have no reason to think it will. He possesses all authority in heaven and on earth to ensure it does not, and, looking into the future two thousand years ago, he made the mighty promise that he will continue to be with his people every day until the end of the age (Matthew 28:18-20). This promise is our guarantee that there will always be those receiving the Word of the kingdom. It is a lifeline to discouraged pastors called to serve in hard areas. Spiritually speaking, they welcome Christ's promise and rejoice to hear accounts of God stretching forth his hand to bless. Humanly speaking, though, it is emotionally challenging to hear of others receiving the tonic of a steady stream of converts, the signs of maturing discipleship, and of the need of extended premises, when your own perennial labors seem to have nothing to show for them.

---

[1] John DeVries (with Todd VanEk and David Stravers), *God's Mission Vision: Pray, Go, Sow, Grow Love* (Grand Rapids: Ephesians 3:20 Publishing, 2018), viii.
[2] Todd M. Johnson and Gina A. Zurlo, eds., *World Christian Database* (Leiden and Boston: Brill), accessed April 2018.
[3] This Pew Forum analysis of data is taken from the Center for the Study of Global Christianity and was published in *Global Christianity* (December 2011).

Although we are drawn instinctively and by the influence of the celebrity culture to lavish attention on the reapers, faithful but unfashionable pastors are comforted that Christ does not forget the sowers. His parable implicitly declares as much.

We might ask why Jesus leaves the seed falling on good soil until last. In each record of the parable this is the case and in none of them does he tell us why. Three suggestions are plausible.

First, a *sociological* suggestion. As we have seen previously, whether we grew up in the church or not, it is typical to spend some time among the crowd before entering the kingdom. It makes sense, then, for Jesus to characterize the rejection of the Word by members of the crowd before noting its acceptance by those becoming citizens of the kingdom. Although we may come into the kingdom at the call of the Word at any time and place, whether by receiving a gospel leaflet through the mail, walking past a public outreach, or hearing "by chance" a message on the radio, it is usual to spend some time in the crowd around Christ before committing to his kingdom.

Regardless, faith in Christ and repentance unto God distinguish citizens of the kingdom from members of the crowd:

- Whereas the crowds are fascinated by Jesus, his disciples are faithful to him. The former observed Christ's miracles, the latter understood they signified that the kingdom had come.

- Whereas the crowds want what Jesus gives, the disciples want Jesus. The former are thankful for the healings and the provisions of the food, the latter prioritize Jesus and make him the main focus of their lives.

- Whereas the crowds forsake Jesus at anytime, the disciples cling to him for time and eternity. The former are fickle and turn away from Jesus once it becomes favorable to do so, the latter understand the sentiment of his first-century disciples: "Lord, to whom shall we go? You have the words of eternal life" (John 6:68).

Second, we may make a *spiritual* suggestion. As true as it is that membership of the crowd typically precedes citizenship of the kingdom, it is even more true to say that the soil of our hearts is poor (like the path, the rocky or thorny ground) unless and until it is transformed into good soil. If Jesus had shuffled his scenarios around and put the case of the seed landing on the good soil amid the cases of the seed landing on the poor soils, we may be forgiven for thinking, leaving aside for the moment the rest of Scripture, that some are born with bad hearts and some with good hearts. However, it is clear from the rest of Scripture that this is not the case.

Each one of us is (mis)shapen (KJV) or brought forth (ESV) in iniquity (Psalm 51:5). In his psalm David is not saying that sex is sinful, but that it can be engaged in in sinful ways (outside of marriage [fornication] or in addition to marriage [adultery]). After all, he is reflecting on his murderous affair with Bathsheba. He says in addition that in some mysterious but very evident way, each person's sin nature is transmitted through their conception.[4] In consequence of this, no one is righteous by nature. We all sin and fall short of God's glory (Romans 3:9-26). We all have, by nature, hearts of poor soil.

While it was not Jesus' intent to tell us in this instance how a heart goes from being bad to good—the parable focuses on the

---

[4] This reality seems to suggest support for the traducianist view over the creationist view of the origin of the soul. In the traducianist view our souls come down to us through the begetting and conception of our parents. While it is a mystery how this occurs, it does account for the fact that we are conceived in sin. It is more difficult to see this if, as in the creationist view, God creates *de novo* each person's soul when they are begotten or conceived.

necessity of conversion (the first three soils) and on the fruit of conversion (this fourth soil)—it is worth our while probing this briefly to ensure that we do not misread or misappropriate the parable. In short, for our hearts to become good, we need to be converted. Although Jesus does not mention conversion in his parable of the sower, the transition from the bad soils to the good soil presumes it. Elsewhere, he spoke of the three constitutive elements of conversion: regeneration (or the new birth), repentance, and faith. It is worth considering these briefly.

The regeneration or new birth which makes possible our actual converting to God is not an explicit theme in the synoptic Gospels. John, however, records Jesus' teaching of it in his Gospel (John 1:12-13; 3:1-8). In regeneration God gives us a new nature. Without one we cannot desire Christ or his kingdom, nor can we repent or entrust our lives to Christ. While we are not conscious of being regenerated (born again or born from above), we are of the repentance and faith which regeneration facilitates. Regeneration, then, is logically prior to repentance and faith, making repentance and faith impossible without a prior regeneration. Regeneration is, accordingly, the foundational subconscious element of conversion and is wrought by the power of God alone. Repentance and faith are its conscious elements and depict our divinely empowered response to God's grace.

Repentance and faith are akin to a one-page (two-sided) passport and, as such, are as necessary for entrance into Christ's kingdom as a passport is to the crossing of a national boundary. On the one side of the page, which is our human response to God, is our repentance and on the other side our faith or believing trust in Jesus (Mark 1:15; cf., Acts 20:21). In the New Testament, these conscious elements of conversion tend to be written of synecdochically. Meaning, that conversion can be spoken of in terms of the command to repent (e.g., Acts 17:30), leaving faith in Christ assumed. After all, repentance is futile unless we believe there is forgiveness in

Christ. Alternatively, conversion is sometimes referred to in terms of the call to trust in Jesus, leaving repentance assumed since faith in Christ is meaningless unless we are convicted of the need to turn from our sins unto God (James 2:5). Repentance and faith are thus distinct but inseparable elements of conversion. Scottish theologian John Murray (1898–1975) stated their relationship beautifully when writing of a penitent faith and a believing repentance.[5]

Note, though, that we are not brought into the kingdom because we bear the passport (repentance and faith/faith and repentance), but because Christ the King has stooped to bear for us the cross. Nevertheless, none of us are brought into Christ's kingdom without conversion. Personal conversion, then, is not the ground upon which we enter the kingdom, it is the occasion on which we do so.

Although the positing of regeneration (the subconscious element of conversion) prior to faith and repentance (the conscious elements) has been questioned in the annals of theological discussion (Augustinians and Calvinists agreeing and Arminians disagreeing), it is not difficult for members of Christ's kingdom to understand that the work of God precedes the response of man. We know very well from experience that prior to coming under the reign of Christ our hearts were hardened, shallow, and/or worldly, and were in need of a divine intervention:

- *Hardened.* Some of us recall very clearly how deliberately we trampled underfoot God's Word or were so careless about its value as to allow the devil to quickly snatch it away.

---

[5] "There is no priority. The faith that is unto salvation is a penitent faith and the repentance that is unto life is a believing repentance" (John Murray, *Redemption—Accomplished and Applied,* reprint ed. [Carlisle, PA: The Banner of Truth Trust, 1979], 113).

- *Shallow.* Some of us know very well what it has been like to make easy, self-centered commitments to Christ. Becoming a Christian was at the time just another of those freebies in life for which we flippantly signed up. Our profession of faith may have been somewhat akin, at least in the British university system, to signing up to an array of clubs during university freshers' week, knowing very well that most of our registrations will come to nothing.

- *Worldly.* Some of us were so busy living for the material and the temporal that we had no time for the Word.

We should not deduce, then, that because Jesus, in the actual parable (in contrast to its interpretation), focused on the responsibility of man rather than the sovereignty of God in salvation, that man responds to the Word out of his own resources. He does not. The good soil is not of his own doing. Christ assumes in this instance the grace of God in the transformation of the soil and the enabling of repentance and faith. His point is not to go into how we are converted, but to underline the necessity of us being so. He would have us say with the apostle Paul, that God the Father "has delivered us from the domain of darkness and transferred us to the kingdom of his beloved Son, in whom we have redemption, the forgiveness of sins" (Colossians 1:13).

Third, there is a *practical* suggestion as to why Jesus speaks of the poor soils before the good soil. He seeks to ensure that his professing disciples are authentic disciples. It is a sobering thought that Judas was, we presume, among the disciples to whom the interpretation of the parable was given. By all appearances, he was a man with a heart of good soil. Not only was he close to Jesus (within the twelve), he served the disciples by keeping the purse (John 13:29). The New Testament records hardly anything of Judas' conversation, but in terms of his presence and involvement, there was no obvious reason why his discipleship would be in question. Events later revealed his heart to be full of thorns. What thorns they must have been to have choked Jesus' preaching for three years! He loved the deceitfulness of riches more than Jesus, even though he was privileged to fellowship with our Lord like few others in history.

Irrespective of the reason or reasons for which Jesus came last to the seed landing on good soil, his concern is the same: to press home what a true Christian looks like. The fact that Jesus was dealing with this issue two thousand years ago, reminds us that the spiritual issues in the background of the parable are perennial. They are intensely relevant to our age. Specifically, this last soil type asks us whether and to what degree our profession of faith in the Lord Jesus is accompanied by the fruit of God's Spirit. His words challenge the cultural "Christian" but are ultimately intended to comfort the true Christian.

THE CHARACTERISTICS OF THE GOOD SOIL

The sower can never adequately or infallibly identify the good soil. We cannot be certain, from appearances, who will respond positively to the Word. Working from what Jesus says of the other soils, we can ascertain certain general aspects of the good soil, but that is all. The work of God is sovereign and mysterious. It defies our finite observational abilities. Hence our rejection of the futility of endeavoring to preach to the elect of God alone. We simply do not know who they are (cf., John 13:1; 2 Timothy 2:19). We thus resist playing God. All we can ascertain is that the soil is softer, moist, and broken up in places.

The soil is softer.

There are several reasons for the softer soil. It has not been trodden endlessly as is the case with the path. Whereas the path has become very compacted and impermeable other than for the network of shallow cracks in the surface, the good soil, being less compacted, has room to breathe. This explains why newcomers to the gospel frequently come to repentance and to faith in the Lord Jesus before those who are gospel hardened. While their hearts, too, are corrupt, they have not become hardened against the gospel by repeated rejection of the command to repent and believe. Their walls are not up like those who anticipate the preacher's personal application of the gospel.

Examples of this irony are plentiful, but one special memory comes to mind. Some years ago, a lady came to Grand Rapids from Iran to visit her family. She had heard from Lili (her daughter) and Rahi (her son-in-law) that they had become Christians but had not seen firsthand what this meant to them. During the first weeks of the visit, Rahi and Lili spoke passionately to her about the gospel, but she wanted none of it. After all, she was Muslim, at least nominally so. They, therefore, determined to say no more of Christ, but to concentrate on living out their faith before her. Intrigued by what she saw, Forough asked to speak with me. After all, I was the closest she knew of to an Imam (teacher in the mosque). Over the next months we met periodically to talk about the gospel, with Rahi and Lili providing the translation and their own input. The visits were exciting, for the Spirit was evidently honoring the burdened prayers of this faithful couple.

In God's providence, Forough's visit was prolonged by challenges to her health. In that time, she went from significant resistance to hearing about Jesus, to proclaiming how she saw light in the faces of the believers she had come to know. By the end of six months, Forough, unable to speak English, nevertheless heard the Word of God and received it. She came before the elders to profess most sincerely her trust in the Lord Jesus and was baptized the Sunday prior to her return to Iran.

Forough was the first converted Muslim to be baptized in, at that time, the one hundred and twenty-three-year history of the church. Lili and Rahi translated her baptismal certificate into Farsi, and we presented her with a Farsi translation of the Bible. I don't think any Western Christians watching on expected the spontaneous gesture which followed. Seventy-five-year-old Forough took the Bible with glee, and looking at it with eyes wide open, kissed it, and held it aloft for all to see. In that one gesture, she demonstrated as clearly as my six years of sermons at the church that the Word of God is the seed of God. Forough was not being bibliolatrous—worshiping Holy Scripture as if the Bible were a fourth person of the Holy Trinity. Nor was she saying in some carnal way that converting to Christianity was a local victory of the Bible over the *Qur'an*. She was giving spontaneous praise to God in her Middle Eastern way for the Word. She was exclaiming in effect that this was the book from which God had spoken to her of his love in Jesus.

I wondered that day, and still do, what onlookers thought who had access to the Word of God all their days and yet remain gospel hardened. Evidently, the devil and his demons, who are neither omnipresent nor omnipotent, failed to get to Forough in time to steal the seed sown in her heart; but they know the gospel hardened through long years of lying to them and distracting them, to such a degree that hardened folk need little help ignoring the Word or trampling it under foot. Not so Forough! New to the message of the gospel, her heart, though as depraved, had, under the influence of God's Spirit, room for the Word of God to grow. There it flourished before she had time to trample it under foot or permit the birds of the air to sweep down to steal it from her.

The soil is moist.

The soil is softer because it remains moist. Whereas in the rocky soil the seed sprung up because of the moisture resting on the rocks under the surface, in the good soil the moisture has seeped

171

down deeper, allowing the seed to develop roots which can better grip the soil. Although it takes longer for the roots to develop, hence the slower upward growth, the stems which germinate are stronger and increase the likelihood of fruit. The seed landing on good soil requires, then, more patience on the part of the farmer. Good farmers are known for this patience. Advises James, "See how the farmer waits for the precious fruit of the earth, being patient about it, until it receives the early and the late rains" (James 5:7).

As we shall see, the wait is worth the while, for the root is the Word which grows in the heart the more it is read and heard. The Word does not bounce off this hearer as it does when the seed lands on the path. Neither is its reach limited by the rocks of hard-heartedness which produces a fake fruitfulness. Nor its growth smothered by the thorns of hedonism in its various forms. Rather, this hearer takes in the Word and nurtures it. Perhaps this nurture begins with the private, even clandestine, reading of the Word. As the roots grow, he or she may, depending on his or her temperament, be emboldened to ask questions of a family member or close friend. Maybe a little bit cryptically at first. Or, the hearer may prefer to sidestep family and friends, taking his or her investigation of Scripture to a minister, elder, or respected member of the church.

Again, my brother comes to mind. More introverted than the rest of us in the family, he was first stirred to study the Scriptures for himself by a remark our father made to him about his spiritual responsibility on the occasion of his becoming a parent. Already getting up earlier than most for work, he later testified how he rose even earlier to read in secret a chapter of the Bible. He did this every day until at last he completed its sixty-six books. Then he started again and read the Bible through a second time. Although a manly ex-soldier, he testified how, when he got to the Book of the Revelation the first time, it terrified him. Yet, by the time he got to it the second time he found it most comforting.

Evidently, the root of the Word had gone deep down into his heart, to the degree that he began to wonder whether he had become a Christian. One wintery day as he walked to work, he received a notable answer from the Lord. Just as he was entering the gateway of his employer's premises, a car slid on the ice, passing his kneecaps within a whisker. He was very close to being injured if not killed. His response was to blurt out, not "Phew, that was lucky!" but "Thank you, Jesus!" In that spontaneous reaction, he realized that he had crossed over into the kingdom, and that God had answered his prayer for assurance that he was now the Lord's.

In terms of the context of the parable, Andy was assured that day by the Lord that he had forsaken the christianese of his life until then for the Christ to which our parents and Sunday School teachers had pointed us. Clearly, the root of the Word had tapped unseen into the waters of regeneration that the Holy Spirit had poured into his otherwise barren heart (cf., Titus 3:5). Now the stem had finally broken through the surface of the soil. This miraculous work of God explains Andy's endurance in getting up at the crack of dawn to read the Word, and the Christ-centered nature of his knee-jerk response to the incident with the car. Whereas earlier he had sat in church as he would have stood to attention on the parade ground—bodily present but mentally, emotionally, and spiritually absent—now he was fully absorbed in seeking God through the study of the Word.

There is a well-known incident in Scripture which speaks to Andy's transformation very well. Recall Lydia who Paul met at Philippi in Macedonia on his second missionary journey. "The Lord," records Luke, "opened her heart to pay attention to what was said by Paul" (Acts 16:14). Evidently, the Lord did the same for Andy. He moistened his heart so that the Word could take root and grow. It continues to do so. Recently, I questioned his replying to my email at 4:35 a.m. He shot back a reply: "Just because I have to start work earlier than usual, the quiet time must not suffer!" Not everyone has such a constitution to be "with it" that early, yet the

Word takes root in the hearts of all those who are authentically citizens of the kingdom of heaven.

It must be said, however, that while there will be fruit for the ministry of the Word, much of the satisfaction of our patience awaits the next life. We live and die in faith, believing that the full harvest of what has been sown will only be seen in the next life. After all, Jesus reminds us in John 4:36-37 that whereas some are called to sow, others are called to reap. Yet, in the afterlife both will rejoice together. This has been the comfort of many laboring away in very difficult circumstances. Reflecting on his field of labor, Paton remarks of the endeavors of the teachers of Aneityumese:

> Doubtless . . . the mighty contrast presented by the life, character, and disposition of these godly Teachers was the sowing of the seed that bore fruit in other days,—though as yet no single Aniwan had begun to wear clothing out of respect to Civilization, much less been brought to know and love the Saviour.[6]

These teachers were serving Christ and his kingdom from the vantage point of time, but God was executing his plans from the vantage point of eternity. Sometimes, then, we shall need more patience than on other occasions to await the fruit of the ministry of the Word. What may be frustrating to us now will, however, occasion our great surprise and joy in the life to come.

The soil is broken up.

Just as the moistening of the soil eases the cultivation of the ground, so the initial influences of the Holy Spirit result in action by the hearer of the Word. Although Jesus makes no specific mention of this, recall again the reference in Hosea to the "breaking up of the fallow ground." Hosea 10:12-13 not only tells us of the need to do

---

[6] *John G. Paton: Missionary to the New Hebrides*, first published 1889; reprint ed. [Edinburgh and Carlisle, PA: The Banner of Truth Trust, 1994), 329.

so, but why. Ephraim had plowed iniquity, reaped injustice, and eaten the fruit of lies. The tribe had trusted in its own way and the multitude of its warriors. Therefore, said the Lord, "Sow for yourselves righteousness, reap steadfast love; break up your fallow ground, for it is time to seek the LORD, that he may come and rain righteousness upon you." A century or more later, Jeremiah spoke similarly to the people of Judah: "Break up your fallow ground, and sow not among the thorns" (Jeremiah 4:3). In the parable then, Jesus, who possessed an authoritative knowledge of the Hebrew Scriptures, was speaking to God's ancient people, teaching them that the thorns are to be torn up, taken away, and burned. This was all part of the process of hoeing the soil in readiness for its plowing.

In the heart of good soil there is, then, a commitment to seek the Lord. The commitment intends a definitive break from sin. This does not mean to say that the person with a heart of good soil is without either original or actual sin. Jesus simply means that we cannot sincerely seek the Lord while yet remaining committed to old transgressions and iniquities. Such orientations are mutually exclusive. We are either sick-to-the-teeth of our sin and stirred thereby to seek the Lord, or we are content in our sin and pay but lip-service at best to seeking him. It is one or the other.

Only in the former scenario can good fruit come forth from the seed of the Word. This principle confirms the truth Jesus had recently conveyed. In the previous chapter Matthew records Jesus' use of a similar picture to teach that good trees bring forth good fruit and bad trees bad fruit (Matthew 12:33-36). From this we glean the truth that the state of our hearts determines what comes forth from them. Without their fallowing, the seed of the Word cannot take root, nor can they bring forth good fruit.

THE ASSESSMENT OF THE FRUIT

It is at this juncture that the difference between the seed sown on the rocky ground and that sown on good soil becomes obvious. Whereas both shoots appear from the ground—the seed from the rocky ground more quickly than the seed from the good soil—it is the latter which lasts and bears grain or fruit.[7] First comes the blade, then the ear, then the full grain in the ear (cf., Mark 4:28). Contrary to the aborted growth of the seed sown on the thorny ground, the seed sown on the good soil has the space and the exterior conditions of sun and rain to grow abundantly.

The difference in the prospect of the seed landing on the different soils lies not in the arm action of the sower (aka the style of the preacher) or in a variant form of seed, but in the blessing of God. The sowing action or preaching is the instrumental means God uses to bring the seed to the soil, but it is the divine preparation of the soil through the work of the Holy Spirit which is the efficient means by which God brings forth the fruit. I refer, theologically, to the Spirit's work of regeneration. All need it to turn to God and to trust in Christ, without exception. Yet, the speed with which the invisible work of the Spirit becomes evident in repentance and faith differs from person to person. Sometimes a regenerate person confesses immediately his or her repentance toward God and trust in Christ. On other occasions the repentance and faith take time to mature in the heart before reaching verbal expression.

The difference may be compared to two light switches, the one clicked on immediately and the other turned on gradually. The conversions of two friends illustrate the difference.

First, there is Jenny. Her conversion, precious regardless of the preacher, occurred under the first evangelistic sermon I preached. If you heard the sermon you would know that this was a miracle! That night in North Wales God was not only teaching Jenny about his power to save, he was reminding me of it, too.

---

[7] Cf., the parable and the interpretation (vv. 8 and 23). The word is the same: *karpos* or fruit.

Following graduation from university and my return to my home church, I had a hunch—with hindsight a prompting of the Holy Spirit—that the leadership would soon ask me to preach. Requesting the Lord to guide me to the passage to use, he placed Matthew 8:28-34 on my heart: the healing of two demon-possessed men. In theory, I believed God could use my immature effort to bring someone to himself, but no one was more shocked (or thrilled) than I when it happened! Following the service Jenny shared with a group of us what God had done for her during the sermon. Truthfully, I oscillated between considerable joy and disbelief. Could it really be that in the course of a single sermon God could translate Jenny from the kingdom of darkness into the kingdom of his Son? It turned out he had, and in the process not only did something wonderful for her, he gave me a sighting of himself as a confirmation of my call to preach. Thirty years later Jenny is going on with the Lord. Whatever was going on in her heart prior to that evening, her response to the Word was immediate. She has not looked back.

Then there is Richard. We had been undergraduate students together but went separate ways after graduating. I went back to North Wales and he went back to London. During the three years together, a few of us had felt for him, befriended him, and witnessed to him. By the time of our graduation, there seemed little to show for the hours spent investing in his life. If anything, Rich, a professing agnostic if not atheist, seemed more critical of Christianity, the church, and of me personally. We spoke a number of times by phone over the following years, but there was no more memorable a telephone conversation than the one two years after graduating in which Rich said he had come to know the Lord. He shared how he had been thinking (and evidently praying) about all the conversations we had had during our days in university. Underneath the surface of his life the Spirit had been transforming the soil of his heart, but it took some time for him to profess his faith in Christ and to identify how God had helped him in his early days as a Christian.

Rich is still going on with the Lord and, the last I heard, was serving as a deacon in his church in London. Praise be to God!

Despite the different ways in which Jenny and Richard came to profess Christ as their King, the Spirit's watering of the Word ensured that roots were put down in their hearts. Although the shoots appeared at different speeds, Jenny's conversion proved that not all immediate conversions are spurious, and Rich's that not all slow responses are nonresponses. From what I recall, Jenny had a lot more previous exposure to the Word than Rich, meaning that her sudden response to the Word was likely a long time in coming. Rich was much newer to firsthand news of the Christian faith, and thus it took longer for the roots of the Word to grip his heart. More important to Jesus is *that* the seed produces fruit than *how long* it takes for the fruit to come forth. It is the fruit and not the shoot that demonstrates the nature of the soil.

The fruit borne.

Although the fruit looks different from the seed which was sown, there is nothing in the fruit which did not find its origin in the seed. So it is with the genuine results of the ministry of the Word. We don't necessarily produce sermons or Bible studies from the Word sown in our hearts, but everything that is produced in and from our hearts through the authentic ministry of the Word finds its origins in the Word.

The parable leads us to the written Word to understand what Jesus has in mind by the fruit. He doesn't tell us exactly, but we know, fundamentally, that he had in mind the necessity of repentance and faith—what we have called the one-page (two-sided) passport needed for admission into the kingdom. Yet, there is more we can say of the fruit than that. The New Testament affords us three main ways of unpacking the idea.

First, there is Jesus' earlier Sermon on the Mount and its countercultural portrayal of kingdom life. The sermon began with the Beatitudes (Matthew 5:1-12). These hallmarks of citizenship in the kingdom we may describe as the fruit issuing from the Word sown in the heart. Whereas those outside the kingdom may and do know moments of joy and laughter, Jesus says that citizens of the kingdom are uniquely blessed. The Greek (*makárioi*) has the idea of serious happiness—a deep-seated joy which is profound not frivolous, and which envelops the deepest sadnesses in life and grants us the capacity to endure them. The blessedness rolls with the fluctuating moods and fortunes of our humanity but is neither absorbed nor extinguished by them. Such robustness or doggedness is attributable to God's Spirit and is rooted in his unchanging character, covenant, and promises.

Not only does this blessedness surpass in depth and longevity the joy and laughter the world has to offer, its dimensions and characteristics also speak of its otherness. I refer to the fact the blessedness of kingdom life is both objective and subjective in nature. Citizens of the kingdom possess an abiding and unchanging blessedness on account of their standing within the kingdom. This standing cannot be taken from us no matter our circumstances or feelings. Yet, our standing within the kingdom makes possible an inner sense of blessedness which ebbs and flows under the influence of various factors, such as our walk with the Lord. It is, however, superior to any joy the world knows, for it is fed by God and is absorbed with him.

"Blessed," Jesus says, "are":

- *"the poor in spirit, for theirs is the kingdom of heaven."* Paradoxically, it is through recognition of our spiritual bankruptcy that we enter the blessings of the kingdom.

- *"those who mourn, for they shall be comforted."* Jesus promises comfort to those truly sorrowful over their sin.

- *"the meek, for they shall inherit the earth."* Although submitting to King Jesus has no natural appeal to us, the sins symptomatic of our spiritual bankruptcy which instill a mournful spirit, also engender the meekness necessary for the glad receiving and serving of Christ. This service is a blessing rather than a drudgery, for it is energized by thoughts of the King and is suffused by his promise that at the fulfillment of the kingdom the new earth shall belong to its citizens.[8]

- *"those who hunger and thirst for righteousness, for they shall be satisfied."* Citizenship in the kingdom of heaven is not simply about ceasing to live in a culture of sin but about yearning for righteousness. Jesus speaks here not of the imputation (or reckoning) of his perfect righteousness to the accounts of his subjects, but of the moral righteousness which develops within us through the rule of Christ over our lives.

- *"the merciful, for they shall receive mercy."* In kingdom life we think not only of ourselves, but of others. Jesus, the merciful King, says there is a blessing attached to being merciful. When we stand before him, those who have been merciful shall receive mercy. Later in the Sermon on the Mount, Jesus affirms this. The measure by which we judge others is that by which we shall be judged (Matthew 7:2). It

---

[8] Dietrich Bonhoeffer makes this very point: ". . . when the kingdom of heaven descends, the face of the earth will be renewed, and it will belong to the flock of Jesus." (*The Cost of Discipleship*, revised and unabridged edition containing material not previously translated [New York: MacMillan Publishing Co., Inc., 1963], 123.)

is, then, for the sake of those we judge as well as for ourselves that we make much of being merciful.

- *"the pure in heart, for they shall see God."* Purity of heart bespeaks the undivided pursuit of God. This purity is important to Jesus because it ensures that we are merciful for the right motives. We are merciful not so as to get into the kingdom, but precisely because we have in God's mercy been already admitted to it. Animated by what we have received from God, we are single-minded in extending to others what we ourselves have received. No matter how much we give out, we are not drained, but are rather sustained by the sight of God—repeated, refreshing sightings of God in this life and uninterrupted personal fellowship with him throughout the ages of eternity to come.

- *"the peacemakers, for they shall be called sons of God."* We cannot, Jesus reasons, pursue God single-mindedly and not be makers of peace on earth. Although Jesus does not countenance peace at the expense of justice or truth, our default position is to pursue the path of peace. We thrive off peace not drama, and thereby demonstrate that we are sons of God or citizens of Christ's kingdom and shall be embraced as such in the consummation.

- *"those who are persecuted for righteousness' sake, for theirs is the kingdom of heaven."* Those possessing the kingdom can expect persecution, but our sufferings only count as persecution when they are for righteousness' sake. When they are, we are not to be ashamed but to rejoice, for the kingdom is ours (cf., 1 Peter 4:16).

These characteristics are not cherry-picked by citizens of the kingdom. Jesus teaches rather that the total package of beatitudes belongs to every citizen of the kingdom, to one degree or another. The Beatitudes distinguish Christ's subjects from the crowds around him and from the world indifferent to him. They are comparable to the fruit of the Word in that they tell us about the context and lives of those belonging to the kingdom.

The Beatitudes qualify as an interpretation of the fruit since they are depictions of the spiritual advantages of admission to the kingdom of heaven. Clearly, Jesus rejects what J. C. Ryle calls "a barren orthodoxy."[9] His view of the fruit is both right and spiritual, and stood in contrast to the political and carnal notion of the kingdom among the religious authorities of his day.

Second, though, is the more anticipated or expected way of unpacking the fruit. That interpretation is given us not by Jesus, but by the apostle Paul. Picking up the idea of fruit, he identifies specific traits emerging in the lives of those having entered the kingdom. Since, by the time he gives his list of fruit in Galatians 5:22-23 the Spirit has come, we are not surprised that he labels the traits "the fruit of the Spirit." Perhaps, it is specifically because the Spirit brings forth the fruit from the seed sown in the hearts of men and women that Jesus held back from identifying the fruit. With his ascension and his sending of the Spirit in his fullness to the church, Paul was able under the inspiration of the Spirit to list the fruit:

- Love.
- Joy.
- Peace.
- Patience.
- Kindness.
- Goodness.
- Faith or faithfulness.

---

[9] J. C. Ryle, *Expository Thoughts on Matthew*, first published 1856 (Carlisle, PA: The Banner of Truth Trust, 1986), 144.

- Gentleness.
- Self-control.

Of this fruit, several observations are noteworthy. First, Paul describes them as a collective (fruit not fruits). Since the fruit is "of the Spirit" we are meant to deduce that in uniting us to Christ—union with Christ being a major theme in Paul's theology—the Spirit ensures that every Christian is enabled to draw from Christ the power to reproduce his virtuous traits. Since we are united to the entire Christ, we can no more cherry pick the fruit of the Spirit than we can the Beatitudes. Thus, every Christian should in some measure exhibit each trait. We do so to different degrees and yet each is present in the life of a citizen of the kingdom. Second, says Paul, we can never have too much of this fruit. There is no restriction limiting our quota, for "against such things [the fruit listed] there is no law." Third, the more fruit we bear the more we make visible the invisible work of the Spirit in blessing to us the Word planted in our hearts (cf., John 15:1-11). Fourth, the fruit is only good if the Christian virtues Paul lists are exhibited in the name of Christ and for the glory of the Father.

Whether we interpret the fruit by the Beatitudes or by the later teaching of Paul, the message is the same. Those who have entered the kingdom are definitively new people. Indeed, Paul warns that if we continue in the works of the flesh we "will not inherit the kingdom of God" (Galatians 5:21). We still sin, that is evident, but sinning is neither our orientation nor our desire. As citizens of the kingdom we now possess a love for God, for his Word, for his people, for holiness of life, and for uprightness in community. Says James our Lord's half-brother, where there is genuine faith in Christ good works substantiate the fact. He asks, "Can a fig tree, my brothers, bear olives, or a grapevine produce figs?" (James 3:12). No, says Jesus in the parable, and evidently James concurs. Like brings forth like. Good soil produces good fruit.

But third, we may unpack Jesus' understanding of the fruit by turning to 2 Peter 1:5-11. There the apostle writes that God has granted us "all things that pertain to life and godliness through the knowledge of [Christ] who called us to his own glory and excellence" (v. 3). He then exhorts those believing in Christ to add to their faith:

- Virtue.
- Knowledge.
- Self-control.
- Steadfastness.
- Godliness.
- Brotherly affection.
- Love.

Very fittingly for our purposes, Peter then adds, "if these qualities are yours and are increasing, they keep you from being ineffective or unfruitful in the knowledge of our Lord Jesus Christ" (v. 8). He goes on to say that it is by nurturing these qualities we make our calling and election sure and that if we practice them—in other words, if we make them part and parcel of who we are in Christ—such qualities will never fall (2 Peter 1:10). Rather, "there will be richly provided for you an entrance into the eternal kingdom of our Lord and Savior Jesus Christ" (v. 11). Peter is not saying that the practice of such qualities will earn us a place in the eternal or consummated kingdom, but that the practice of them demonstrates that we are, by grace, already members of the kingdom to be fulfilled when Christ returns.

Whether we understand the grain or fruit in the parable in terms of the Beatitudes (drawing from Jesus), the fruit of the Spirit (drawing from Paul), or the virtues added to faith (drawing from Peter), it is clear that the produce has more in view than the initial repentance and faith occasioning our entrance into the kingdom. It also is more fundamental than our works as Christians, for it develops not from law (although it comports with it) but from the life and love of Christ. Asks Andrew Murray in one place: "Have you ever noticed the difference in the Christian life between work and fruit. A machine can do work; only life can bear fruit." And yet, we could not know of Christ apart from the preaching of the Word. Thus, the idea of fruit redresses the opposing imbalances of lawlessness and legalism.

In the celebrity and consumerist culture of our day, there are those stressing the freedom of the Christian, pitting the life of the Spirit within against the law of God given us from without. Yet, even the Spirit, if I may put this reverently, needs an objective standard or standards by which to lead us into holiness. Of course, these standards he, as a member of the Godhead, originates and applies. We can refer generally to that standard as the moral law (the Ten Commandments) which we have seen has an abiding role in this new covenant era and in the Christian's life in structuring our freedom in Christ. Or we can refer to those specific standards germane to the parable, whether we reference the Beatitudes, the fruit of the Spirit, or the virtues added to faith. Whichever way we look at the fruit, citizens of the kingdom, granted hearts of good soil, have a duty, desire, and empowerment to demonstrate that their lives have been divinely and graciously transformed.

Conversely, there is the opposing danger of a reactionary legalism which so stresses the abiding relevance of the moral law as to forget that being a Christian is fundamentally a life lived in Christ and out of his resources. Fruit grows from the seed planted in the heart precisely because there is life at work to produce it. The life that the citizen of the kingdom lives, he lives by the power of the Spirit, from the virtue of Christ, and unto the Father's glory.

The balanced life of the citizen of Christ's kingdom is, then, a matter of both *being* and *doing*. On the one hand we guard against a pietism which can be all about me and my holiness but AWOL when it comes to serving in the church, reaching out to neighbors with the gospel, defending the faith, or appealing for justice in society. On the other hand, we check ourselves when we:

- Make more of our resumés than of our conformity to Christ.
- Revel in our productivity and busyness at the expense of glorying in the Lord.
- Treat others around us as if they exist to help us build our kingdom rather than as fellow citizens united in pursuit of Christ's glory and honor.

To ignore the need for self-examination is not only to allow a rot to set into the fruit envisioned by the Word, it is to buy into a worldly evolutionary mindset which places value on how much a person contributes, rather than on their likeness to Christ. Citizens of the kingdom are not *automata* but living entities rooted in Christ for communion with the living God.

The fruit measured.

Observes John De Vries, "A farmer does more than plant seed. He grows, harvests, and measures the crop. We are called to do the same."[10] Whether Jesus intends us to go as far as Mission India in documenting results—the assiduousness among colleagues on the subcontinent is said to have been a hangover from British rule—Jesus evidently has results in mind since the seed landing on good soil is said to produce thirtyfold, sixtyfold, or a hundredfold. Although it is uncertain as to how far we can press Jesus' meaning, three things are clear.

First, that wherever the seed lands on the good soil there produce will develop. Indeed, there is no membership of the kingdom without fruit emerging from the living and abiding Word of God (cf., 1 Peter 1:23).

Second, no matter how good the sower is in sowing the seed as evenly as he can, it will be unevenly productive. It brings forth

---

[10] DeVries, *God's Mission Vision*, 58.

fruit, some thirtyfold, some sixtyfold, and some a hundredfold. Different factors determine the amount of fruit we bear. While each of us knows seasons of growth and faces particular God-ordained providences which shape our opportunities for growth and for service, there are nevertheless factors common to all citizens of the kingdom which determine the degree to which we produce fruit. Here are three of them:

- *Factor #1: Faithfulness.* Our commitment to the personal and communal means of grace and our readiness to listen to God speaking through his Word, will tell over the long haul. The fruit develops not simply through meditation, but, to quote Eugene Peterson's definition of discipleship, through "long obedience in the same direction" (meaning, the right direction).[11] "As Christ is the root by which a saint grows," observes another writer, "so is he the rule by which a saint walks."

- *Factor #2: Giftedness.* It is evident that God has given a greater allotment of gifts to one believer than to another. Perhaps a better mind than others to see heart-stirring truths; or greater facility of speech to communicate accessibly and attractively; or more efficiency for the organizing of the work of ministry; etc. Even among those with similar gift sets there is variation in the degree of gifting. Yet, unless it is exercised faithfully, it will always be possible for one Christian, less greatly endowed than another, to produce more fruit than the one receiving from the Spirit the greater gift.

---

[11] Eugene H. Peterson, *A Long Obedience in the Same Direction: Discipleship in an Instant Society,* Christian Basics Bible Studies, first published 1980 (Downers Grove, Illinois: InterVarsity Press, 2000).

- *Factor #3: Opportunity.* No Christian is more saved than another. We have either entered the kingdom and are citizens of it or we have not. Nevertheless, the longer we follow Christ the more opportunity is ours to grow fruit. How wonderful it is to meet believers, well-past their physical prime, exhibiting the fruit that lasts. Now weak in their bodies, they yet exude strength. Their inner man grows stronger by the day (2 Corinthians 4:16; cf., Ephesians 3:16). They have made the King and his kingdom their passion and preoccupation, and it tells. Thus, even as their lives of service draw to a close, the fruit they bear is seen in what they are. The thief on the cross who turned to God through Christ in his dying moments was as much a citizen of the kingdom as is its longest serving member, yet he had no time or opportunity to add to his repentance and faith. In the seed of the Word received from Christ lies the potential for every fruit of the Spirit, for they are all bound together in Christ, but the converted thief had no opportunity to show the amount or array of fruit that comes from the good soil. We remember him for his repentance and faith, but not for his subsequent life of obedience or his works of service. In doctrinal terms, he was definitively sanctified, and, in paradise, we can expect to find him finally or perfectly sanctified, but there is neither record nor evidence of the progressive sanctification which typifies the lives of Christ's disciples here on earth.

Third, although perhaps less clearly, Jesus may well have in mind the impact of the growth of his disciples on those around them. Obviously, the thirty*fold*, sixty*fold*, and hundred*fold* has immediate reference to the superabundance of grain or fruit issuing from every seed planted in the good soil. Many virtues and good deeds come from each conversion. Yet, as disciples of Christ we also multiply ourselves. Some self-multiply minimally, some self-multiply moderately, and some self-multiply greatly. Jesus is likely thinking, then, not only of the increase of our individual qualities as his disciples, but of the increase of the kingdom. After all, the parable of the sower is the first in his series which includes those alluding to the growth of the kingdom, such as the parable of the mustard seed, the leaven, and even the parable of the net (Matthew 13:31-33, 47-50).

Coming to mind in connection with this self-multiplication are biblical references to the grain dying, the seed falling in the ground, and producing a further crop of its own. Jesus spoke in these terms of his own death: "Truly, truly, I say to you, unless a grain of wheat falls into the earth and dies, it remains alone; but if it dies, it bears much fruit" (John 12:24). Similarly, the apostle Paul, writing of the bodily resurrection of God's people, anticipates the question "How are the dead raised?" To which he answers, "You foolish person! What you sow does not come to life unless it dies. And what you sow is not the body that is to be, but a bare kernel, perhaps of wheat or of some other grain" (1 Corinthians 15:36-37).

Reflecting on these cross-references in light of the parable of the sower, it may be said that we serve the extension of the kingdom of heaven by our dying. Spiritually speaking, the seed of the Word sown in our hearts causes us to die to self. This is a component of our surrendering to Christ. Yet, physically speaking, the seed of the Word may result down the road in our death by persecution for righteousness' sake. History is replete with examples of how Christians who, through death to self, died for Christ, were in fact used of God to spread his kingdom. It is feasible, then, that when Jesus speaks of our bringing forth fruit, thirtyfold, sixtyfold, or a hundredfold, he not only had in mind the subsequent lives of his apostles and disciples, but, in one way or another, also their deaths.

CONCLUSION

It is doubtful whether Jesus means us to press his parable further in terms of measuring the crop. As for our being, who other than God can quantify our growth in grace? As for doing, who is able to quantify accurately the works we undertake for the Lord? We can advertise how many articles and books we have written, how many radio stations our ministries are aired on, how big are the budgets of our churches—all features of American Christianity rather than of the kingdom of God—but at the end of the age our works are going to be tested by fire. That which is reduced to rubble will not count in the final reckoning (1 Corinthians 3:12-15). Some of the brands and kingdoms we so laud will not look so impressive from the vantage point of eternity, and some of the unknown servants and uncelebrated ministries deemed as uncool or unfashionable, and which we have overlooked or even pooh-poohed, will, to our humble acknowledgement, be embraced by Christ as silver and gold.

Jesus' main point, then, is not to measure the fruit exactly, but to say that his true disciples will inevitably bring forth fruit and that we are called to bring forth much of it. Even minimal fruit is thirtyfold! Such a challenge to us from the parable of the sower is confirmed by Jesus' teaching in John's Gospel. Whereas the synoptic Gospels record Jesus' parables, John records Jesus' "I am" sayings. Especially relevant from John's record of Jesus' "I am" sayings is his declaration to be the true vine. It is fitting to allude to this saying in relation to the synoptics' record of the parable of the sower since they supplement each other. The former enables us to remember that our subjection to the reign of Christ is not one of formality and of humiliation but of fellowship with him in his royalty.

Three points Jesus makes in regard to his claim to be the true vine are germane to the parable of the sower.

First, Jesus forewarns us that whoever does not bring forth fruit, he takes away (John 15:2). In other words, we can exhibit all the christianese we like, but unless we bear the fruit of the Spirit we cannot authentically claim to belong to Christ. In the current climate we may add, neither can we claim to be a Christian if we redefine what Jesus means by fruit. Think of the person who promotes, in the name of Christian love, politically correct views at odds with the word of Christ and insists on doing so even after having been shown from Scripture his or her error. Or, the person who, again in the name of Christ, so focuses on worthy buzz themes such as care for the environment, the plight of the pre-born, or a just foreign policy but neglects the necessity of God's saving grace and a holy life. My point is not to advocate a narrow-minded, self-centered brand of pietism indifferent to the issues of the day, but to stress that as important as these are, there can be no fruit from the seed of the Word where there is no basic concern for *pietas* (personal devotion to God).

Second, we are not to be satisfied with producing fruit. As in the parable of the sower, so in Jesus' claim to be the true vine, we are called to bring forth *much fruit*. "By this my Father is glorified," says Jesus, "that you bear much fruit and so prove to be my disciples" (John 15:8). Indeed, Jesus ensures that we bear much fruit: ". . . every branch that does bear fruit, he prunes that he may bear more fruit" (John 15:2).

Negatively speaking, bringing forth more fruit entails breaking the patterns of habitual sin. Since, says John in 1 John 3:9, God's seed abides in us we cannot keep on sinning.[12] Rather, we must mortify sin, which is to say that we must put it to death or stamp it out. Positively speaking, we are to proactively pursue holiness in our lives. In his "I am" saying, Jesus says we bring forth

---

[12] In 1 John the imagery behind the idea of seed is that of sperm and comports with the apostle's depiction of the new birth.

fruit by abiding or remaining in Christ. The idea follows on from that of the engrafting of the branch into the vine. In the parable of the sower by contrast, the fruit hangs from its own shoot. Despite the pictorial difference, the principle, stated implicitly in the parable but explicitly in the "I am" saying, is the same. Namely, that there can be no fruit unless there is a vital connection to the life-giving apparatus of the plant or vine. Conversely, by the power of the life of Christ we bring forth much of it (John 15:5). We do so through intimate spiritual fellowship with Christ, in the context of which we delight to pursue the fruit of godliness, of Christlikeness, and of holiness.

Fruitfulness is not an option. Christ says that if anyone does not abide in him he is thrown away like a branch and withers; and the branches are gathered, thrown into the fire, and burned (John 15:6). In the final analysis, then, it is not a professing of faith in Christ which distinguishes citizens of the kingdom from members of the crowd, but holiness of life. It is not conversion *in se*, but our transformation. The more fruit we bear, the more undoubted is the authenticity of our Christianity.

Yet, the fact that we live in the true vine and are to abide in him reminds us that we pursue his pleasure and serve his kingdom not as those under forced labor, but as those whose greatest honor on earth is to know the King and to belong to his kingdom. I think, by way of example, of Graham and Colin, two erstwhile servants of the British royal household once known to our family. We can learn from them. Never did we hear them complain of being servants of her majesty. I remember rather their loyalty, contentment, and sense of honor, their discretion too. Simply put, they were ever mindful of whom they represented. If that was how they served at Buckingham Palace, how much greater our privilege in serving the King of kings and Lord of lords. Christianese then, or Christ? To the authentic disciple of Christ, this is a question not worth asking. There is no comparison.

STUDY QUESTIONS: SESSION SEVEN

1. Have you ever thought, "Does *anybody* receive the seed of God's Word?" What factors drove you to ask the question, and how did you answer it?

2. If we treat the parable wrongly, with "strict scientific accuracy," we would think Jesus teaches that there are hearts which are naturally good. What is it about the character and the records of the parables and the theology of Scripture which counters this thinking?

3. Since the LORD alone knows those who are his, how did we deduce from the parable how to identify the good soil?

4. What experiences can you share of conversions, whether of your own or of someone else's, which attest to the characteristics of the good soil?

5. What factors have especially impacted for good or bad your yielding of fruit as a citizen of the kingdom of heaven?

6. How would you present a case for embracing Christ as King to someone outside the kingdom of heaven?

Prayer: Lord, we bring to you those servants of yours discouraged by little sight of the fruit of the Word, even as we praise you for those areas of the world where the kingdom of heaven is growing tremendously. Grant encouragement and inspiration on the one hand and humility and sound teaching on the other. For the glory of your name we ask these things, through Jesus Christ our Lord. Amen.

In preparation for the Afterword, read: John 6:22-71.

AFTERWORD
CHRISTIANESE OR CHRIST?

He who has ears, let him hear.
Matthew 13:9; cf., Mark 4:9, Luke 8:8b.

Sometimes a book, a film, or a play leaves us hanging, wondering what happened to the main characters. On other occasions, we are provided with snippets of information summarizing how things unfold thereafter. The author or director decides the ending—whether to leave the reader or viewer tantalized, at liberty to envision their own ending, or whether to tie the knots of the story. I opt for the latter, narrating how the question "Christianese or Christ?" was answered in the first century A.D. and asking how we answer it today. This is no light matter. In his earnestness about the kingdom, Jesus went on to teach another six parables underlining the vital necessity of belonging to it and of living out its values (Matthew 13:24ff.).

HOW THE APOSTLES ANSWERED

To a degree this is obvious. We wouldn't be considering Christ's parable were it not for the apostles' God-given submission to his reign, their faithful preaching of the word of the kingdom, and the fruit of holiness they bore along the way. Neither their mature knowledge of Christ nor their consistent submission to his reign came overnight. Initially they needed the interpretation of the parable and revealed on times throughout our Lord's ministry how slow they were to learn. So much so that we might be forgiven for wondering why Jesus did not delay his return to heaven.

He did not for at least two reasons. First, Jesus anticipated the massive learning curve that his resurrection would initiate. In the forty days which followed his return to life, he had ample time to show how his resurrection brought together the pieces of his ministry. Daily, the apostles must have said to Jesus, "Ah, I get it now!" Second, Jesus' ascension, followed ten days later by his empowerment of the apostles by the Spirit, would complete their training. With the knowledge Jesus imparted in person and the power he bestowed on them by his sending of the Holy Spirit, they were ready to spread the kingdom from Jerusalem, to all Judea, to Samaria, and to the uttermost parts of the known world (Acts 1:8). From Pentecost onward, the Holy Spirit, the representative of Christ on earth, would encourage, guide, and teach the apostles how to tear down the strongholds of Satan and to build the kingdom of the Lord Jesus. As Christ had remarked in his Farewell Discourse (John 14–16): "I still have many things to say to you, but you cannot bear them now. When the Spirit of truth comes, he will guide you into all truth, for he will not speak on his own authority, but whatever he hears he will speak, and he will declare to you the things that are to come" (John 16:12).

Ministering in the afterglow of Pentecost, not only as those baptized with the Spirit but as those repeatedly filled with him (e.g., Acts 2:4; 4:31), the apostles witnessed firsthand the truth of Jesus' parable. There was good fruit to be seen across the east of the Roman Empire with the Word about to reach the West by the completion of the canon of Scripture (Romans 15:22-24). Yet, not even in those days did the seed always fall on good soil. Think of the arrest in Jerusalem of Peter and John by the Sanhedrin, and of the killing of James by Herod (Acts 4:1-22; 12:1-5); of Paul, on his first missionary journey, being left for dead in Lystra (Acts 14:19-20); or, on his third missionary journey, of his abandoning of teaching in the synagogue in Ephesus due to the stubbornness of the Jews (Acts 19:8-9); and of his arrest and eventual imprisonment in Rome (Acts 21:27–28:31). We could go on.

The apostles preached Christ with their lives as well as with their lips, and in a way of which Christ would approve. It had not always been so. Think back on their scattering in fear at the time of

Jesus' arrest, with Peter going so far as to deny his Lord (Matthew 26:69-75; Mark 14:66-72; Luke 22:54-62; John 18:15-18, 25-27). Recall also that it was the women and not the apostles who were first to the tomb on the resurrection morn (Matthew 28:1-10; Mark 16:1-8; Luke 24:1-12; John 20:1). Nevertheless, under the apostles' watch the kingdom not only spread throughout the known world it became renowned for the very virtue Jesus had promoted in his new commandment, namely, reciprocal love (John 13:31-35). Their agapaic or self-sacrificing love was inspired by the unrivaled expression of it they had seen in Christ and was empowered by the Holy Spirit shedding abroad within them the love of God (Romans 5:5). It became visible not only in the way they loved one another, but in their loving of the lost. Indeed, all but one of the post-Judas band of apostles gave their lives for Christ and for the cause of his kingdom. John, the apostle of love, was exiled for some time on the Isle of Patmos (Revelation 1:9) but died in old age of a nonviolent death.

But neither the apostles' salvation nor admission to the kingdom of heaven lay in their apostleship. Judas clearly demonstrates this. King David foretold of his betrayal (Acts 1:16), and Jesus knew of it ahead of time (John 6:70-71). He told Judas that he should go and do what he had planned to do (Luke 22:21-23; especially John 13:1-30). Judas reminds us solemnly that no amount of time spent around Jesus substitutes for union with him and for submission to him. It bears repeating that the crowds came and went, but Judas daily ate with Jesus, talked with him, heard his discourses, observed his miracles, and was even entrusted with the communal money bag. Looking back on Judas' apostleship, Peter could say that, "he was numbered among us, and was allotted his share in this ministry" (Acts 1:17). Yet, Judas never entered Christ's kingdom. Instead, for thirty pieces of silver he obtained for the religious hierarchy of Israel what they, as the authorities, had been unable to procure for themselves, namely, a way to arrest Jesus.

It was because Judas never submitted to Christ's rule over his life that the devil could put into his heart the desire to betray Jesus (John 13:2). It is so obvious with hindsight that Judas had a heart like the thorny ground. Jesus had sowed into him the seed of the kingdom for three years and yet the thorns choked it. The rest, as they say, is history. Full of remorse for facilitating Jesus' condemnation, Judas returned to the chief priests and elders, confessing to them that he had sinned by betraying innocent blood. Faced with their callous indifference to his heartache and their culpability, Judas threw down the thirty pieces of silver in the temple and went and hung himself (Matthew 27:3-5). Evidently his "change of mind" was emotional; we may even call it repentance since Matthew uses one of the Greek words for it (*metamelomai*). This repentance, while sorrowful, was a carnal and not a Godly repentance. Whereas the one is self-centered and leads to despair and to death, the other is God-centered and leads to Christ and to hope. Thus, a field was bought with the proceeds of the betrayal. It became known as the "Field of Blood" (cf., Matthew 27:3-10; Acts 1:18-19).

Thinking back on the apostles, we see clearly two important lessons.

First, that there is a world of difference between Christ and christianese. What a contrast between the maturing surrender of those apostles subject to Christ and the self-interest of Judas. There have been those who have sought to recover Judas as a long-lost saint of the church, but to no avail. A fellow student during my postgraduate studies, who was very prominent among the student body, was one such proponent of the idea. Suddenly he vanished. Upon inquiry as to his whereabouts, I was told that he had sat his viva for his doctorate, but the examiners, against the flow of this age of absurdities, had found his thesis to be unsustainable.

Second, when we recall that Judas held office in the church—the extraordinary but temporary office of apostle (cf., Ephesians 2:20 and 4:11-12)—we are reminded that today's officebearers also face the challenge as to whether we truly belong to Christ. How many Judases in the professing church are betraying Jesus today to those who would crucify and rid society of him? This is what is happening when leaders in the church capitulate to society instead of calling men and women in their communities to repentance toward God and faith in our Lord Jesus Christ. Evidently, the world ignores the call to embrace Christ as Savior and King from the lips of those who betray him for their own convenience. As Peter later wrote, "it is time for judgment to begin at the household of God; and if it begins with us, what will be the outcome for those who do not obey the gospel of God?" (1 Peter 4:17).

HOW THE DISCIPLES ANSWERED

Christ's disciples were admitted to the kingdom through a penitent and believing response to Jesus' Word. Yet, their experience of admission differed from ours today. Whereas they straggled the old and new covenant eras, we belong solely to that of the new covenant. Thus, there was a time lag between their repentance and faith on the one hand and their Holy Spirit baptism on the other. At the point at which they turned to God and rested in Christ, Christ had not yet been glorified, and was not, therefore, positioned at the right hand of the Father to send the Spirit in his fullness (John 7:37-39). Thus, their Holy Spirit baptism awaited the day of Pentecost (Acts 2:38). In the meantime, they had enough of the Spirit for the desire and empowerment to repent and believe, but not so much of him as to weld them together with believing Gentiles into one body of believers (equally subject to Christ) and to propel them out in the world of nations with power to spread the kingdom.

The three thousand converted on the day of Pentecost were the first ones to have both their feet in the new covenant era. Accordingly, their Holy Spirit baptism coincided with their repentance and faith, as per Peter's promise in Acts 2:38. Pentecost signaled the fact that from henceforth conversion would become a one-moment or movement experience in which Holy Spirit baptism and repentance and faith, while distinct, would go hand in hand as part of each conversion. Thus, from the day of Pentecost onward, Christ's original disciples and those newly made disciples proceeded onward together. They were all baptized once-for-all with the Spirit but needed to be filled and refilled with the Spirit to accomplish the spread of Christ's kingdom (Acts 2:4; 4:8, 31; 6:3, 5 [cf., 7:55]; 9:17; 11:24; 13:9, 52).

Christ's true disciples proved to be an invaluable help to the apostles in supporting the work of the kingdom. After the persecution broke out in Jerusalem, it was the disciples rather than the apostles who were scattered abroad, spreading the gospel as they went (Acts 8:1, 4). The KJV states that they "preach[ed] the Word." Such was their excitement on account of what Christ meant to them, they, in effect, gossiped the gospel wherever they went. Once the missionary journeys got under way and churches were planted, the authentic disciples of Christ provided the necessary pastors and teachers, evangelists, elders and the deacons, and congregants. Eternity will declare how many of these officebearers and the rank and file of Christ's disciples gave their lives in the cause of Christ and his kingdom. They demonstrated the truth of Pastor Richard Wurmbrand's words: "A man really believes not what he recites in his creed, but only the things he is willing to die for."[1]

Not every professing disciple of Christ, though, turns out to be authentic. In every generation there are professing disciples who,

---

[1] *The Voice of the Martyrs*, Special Issue, 2018.

inwardly, remain but members of the crowd around Jesus. They can recite the Apostles' Creed but would not contemplate dying for the God it depicts. John substantiates this. He tells us not only of such subsequent signs of the kingdom as the feeding of the five thousand (John 6:1-13), but of the conversation which followed: "When the people saw the sign that he had done, they said, 'This is indeed the Prophet who is to come into the world!'" (v. 14). They recognized not only Christ's prophethood but, additionally, his kingship, for they then sought by force to make him King. Where they erred was in their belief that Christ could be made a political monarch when, in fact, he was already a spiritual one. Their political and material concept of his kingship was not his, nor was he prepared to allow it to stir an inevitable response from Rome or to distract him from his establishment of the kingdom of heaven. Thus, Jesus withdrew alone to the mountain to pray.

Doubtless, it was his communion with his Father on the mountain which determined his response to the growing crowds. Fresh from his consultation with his Father, Jesus came down from the mountain ready to emphasize to the crowds the primary importance of their entrance into the kingdom of heaven. This fresh intent was not a contradiction of what he had taught to date, but a heightening of his focus on the spiritual needs before him. The time had come for them to decide what to do with him and with his message. Thus, Christ ratcheted up his royal claim over lives, not only to indict the crowds for not having come under his reign but to distinguish his true disciples from those who were fake.

By the time Jesus had descended the mountain, the apostles had made their way across the Sea of Galilee to the other side. Having caught up with them by walking on the water, Jesus and his apostles arrived immediately at the other side (John 6:14-21). Not until the next day did the crowds realize that Jesus has crossed over to Capernaum. Following suit, they ask Jesus upon their arrival, "Rabbi, when did you come here?" (John 6:25). Jesus answered them rather bluntly: "Truly, truly, I say to you, you are seeking me, not because you saw the signs, but because you ate your fill of the loaves" (John 6:26). Explains Farrar, "It was not [Christ's] object to become the centre of an admiring populace, or to spend His whole time in working miracles, [for] though they were deeds of mercy, [they] were mainly intended to open . . . hearts to His diviner teaching".[2] Thus, rather than pander to the crowds, Jesus tells them in effect, "You are here for the wrong reason!" Directing their focus back to the primacy of their spiritual needs, he describes himself as "the bread of life" they need most of all. "As physically hungry as you are," he said in paraphrase, "your spiritual needs are weightier." Thus, Jesus corroborated why he began earlier to speak in parables. He was signaling the impending judgment on those who heard the Word but did not listen to it.

Not content with Jesus' thinking, and conscious of his lowly origins in Nazareth, the Jews began to grumble about him (John 6:41). Undaunted, Jesus persevered with his teaching, declaring that he is the bread come down from heaven so that those believing in him will live forever. As was typical, his claim divided the crowds. Perplexed as to *how* they could eat his flesh to live eternally, Jesus emphasizes to them *that* they must eat: "Truly, truly, I say to you, unless you eat the flesh of the Son of Man and drink his blood, you have no life in you. Whoever feeds on my flesh and drinks my blood has eternal life, and I will raise him up on the last day" (v. 53).

John records not that the *crowds* could stomach Jesus' teaching no longer, but that "many of his *disciples* [italics inserted]" could not. They responded, "This is a hard saying; who can listen to it?" (v. 60). Jesus, aware of the grumbling, insisted his words are spirit and life, but was not surprised at having to do so. Note John's editorial comment: "For Jesus knew from the beginning who those

---

[2] Frederic W. Farrar, *The Life of Christ*, "The Quiver" Edition (London, *et al.*: Cassell, 1896), 171.

were who did not believe, and who it was who would betray him (v. 64). As if to prove Jesus' assessment, he then adds, "many of his disciples [also *mathētōn*] turned back and no longer walked with him" (v. 66).

It is because of the disciples' reaction that I have belabored the point that not all who claimed to be Christ's disciples were in fact such. Here we are some way down the road from Jesus' parable of the sower, discovering that some of his disciples (read, professing disciples) turned away from Jesus and walked no more with him. We are not to understand by this that they fell from grace, but that they were not true disciples in the first place. They possessed christianese but not Christ. But there is more.

Contrary to today's fixation with numbers, Jesus let them go. Yes, you read that aright. He let them go! They had been with him long enough to make up their minds as to whether they were going to take him on his own terms and to live under his reign. In turning away, they voted with their feet. Had Jesus run after them he would have overridden their personal responsibility to truly repent and believe and he would have treated them as *automata* or machines rather than as the free agents they were created to be.[3] Jesus would also have demeaned his kingdom in the process, conveying the impression that it desperately needs more subjects, and that those who won't enter the kingdom willingly need to be press-ganged to do so.

---

[3] It would greatly help in theological discussion to distinguish man's free agency from free will. Man is a free agent capable of practical choice, but at the Fall he lost his free will. His moral choices are bound in sin, such that he either actively pursues sin or is unable to perform any works that are truly good (done in the name of Christ and for the glory of God). That is, until or unless he is regenerated or born again, by which we mean he is given a new nature, capable of, and willing to glorify God by undertaking works done in the name of Jesus Christ.

Since Christ refused to lower the standards of discipleship in order to extend his reign, so must we. Our goal in this celebrity-driven age is not to pursue ever greater numbers at all costs, but to faithfully echo Jesus' loving call to repentance and to faith and to uphold the countercultural standards of the kingdom that he has established with royal authority. Naturally, we pray the kingdom of heaven will spread, but we are not responsible for those who have heard the Word of the Kingdom but have continually rejected it (cf., Ezekiel 3:16-22). The authentic growth of the kingdom is conditioned on the terms established by King Jesus and not by us. When we alter what Christ has clearly stated concerning entrance into the kingdom and life in the kingdom, we enlarge not Christ's kingdom but one of our own viewpoint and making.

Jesus' readiness to let go those appearing to be his disciples likely confused his hearers. After all, part of his appeal to the crowds lay in his ability to draw them. Likewise, Jesus' readiness goes against the grain of many a celebrity pastor's psyche, too. If they were to buy into Jesus' philosophy of ministry and thin out the crowds by refusing to excise Jesus' hard sayings from their preaching, or to limit the application of them to what is noncontroversial, and forwent following up with those turning away from their preaching, they could well be ostracized by at least some congregants as proverbial bulls in china shops, and quite possibly subjected to an eldership review of their ministry. The possibility of being fired for want of winsomeness and diplomacy is real. "We want a pastor who will draw the people, not offend them!" would go up the cry.

Now doubtless, pastors can speak out of turn. We do not have faultless emotional intelligence, we face unseen pressures, and are called to expound scriptures which are unpalatable to the natural man. Yet, before deducing that your pastor is to blame for declining numbers (supposing that to be the case), compare his ministry to that of the prophets and ultimately to that of Jesus. Not the mythically mild Jesus of the children's chorus, but the principled Jesus of the Gospels. Pastors suffer when their ministries are compared to a distorted caricature of our Lord. The fact of the matter is that, notwithstanding Jesus' fullness of grace, his preaching proved to be an offence to many. It served not only to bring men and women into the kingdom but to help others determine that his kingdom was not for them. Once he deduced that those with ample opportunity to hear his message cast off their claims to be his followers, he let them go. He did so to focus on those willing to receive him and his teaching. There comes a point in our interactions when we must do so, too.

At least the false disciples were consistent. Once they decided they didn't like what Jesus had to say they followed him no more. Better that than the situation we have today, in which those not liking Jesus' hard sayings try to rebrand him and to get his followers to chase after the caricature rather than the reality of who he is. The question the subsequent history of the disciples raises, then, is this: Are we true or false disciples? One way to tell is whether we find ourselves offended by ministers who expound the Scriptures on their own terms, and whether we are willing to grapple in humility with the hard sayings of Jesus. The church, specifically her leadership, has a responsibility to supply well-meant questions with substantive and biblically substantiated answers, yet she has no call from Christ to empower those who would reject him and his Word. Nor is the church duty bound to run after those bent on such rejection. To expect otherwise is characteristic consumerism.

HOW THE CROWDS ANSWERED

Immediately, the crowds responded to Christ's kingship and his offer of the kingdom of heaven with indifference. Ultimately, however, they responded with hostility. This we might expect, for we can never remain indifferent to Christ, no matter how long we fain it. Either we eventually surrender to him, or we become his implacable foes.

It is in reference to the crowds that Matthew goes on to record in his thirteenth chapter that Jesus said "nothing to them without a parable." It is hard to imagine that Matthew means us to understand this absolutely, as if to say that Jesus never again taught the crowds in anything other than in parables. In actuality, Matthew's Gospel records from here on out little of Jesus' teaching of the crowds. We read of the feeding of the five and four thousands, of Jesus' compassion on account of their hunger and, on other occasions, of their sicknesses. But we do not read explicitly that he taught them, let alone that he did so exclusively in parables. Interestingly, in the later instances in the Gospel of Jesus' teaching, it is the disciples (Matthew 18:1, 10-14, 21-35; 20:1-16; 24:3 and 25:1-30) and the religious hierarchy (Matthew 21:23–22:14) to whom the parables are directed. We read nothing of the crowds being taught by means of them. When at last we read of Jesus addressing them once more, he went without parables to do so (Matthew 23:1-38). It seems more likely, then, that Jesus spoke nothing but parables to the crowds in this recorded episode of his ministry. He did so, as we know, to fulfill prophecy (Matthew 13:35) and to draw a line though the crowd, distinguishing those belonging to the kingdom from those yet outside it.

For all that the parables signified the impending judgment on the crowds, they continued to enjoy Christ's general benevolence. They received food, healings, and warnings of the dead religion and gross hypocrisy of the religious authorities (Matthew 14:14, 34-36; 15:32; 23:1-38). The signs of the kingdom, then, were not conditional upon personal repentance and faith. They were born out of Jesus' general love for the masses, notwithstanding their rejection of his kingship and kingdom, and were a witness to its arrival. Nevertheless, with the privilege of witnessing the signs came an increasing culpability for not receiving Christ. It was theirs to reason that if Christ could feed them physically, he could feed them spiritually; if he could heal them bodily, he could heal their souls;

and if he could denounce dead religion, he could guarantee them a living relationship to God.

The crowds following Jesus were, of course, a fluid entity. The individuals making up the crowd differed from day to day. While they followed Jesus from Galilee to Judea (Matthew 19:1-2), it is unrealistic to assume that they were entirely the same as had followed him in the north of the land and were awaiting him in Jerusalem upon his arrival there. Our interest in the crowds, then, is not in a fixed set of individuals but in a commonly held mindset we have labeled *christianese*. One of the prime features of christianese is its fickleness, hence the crowds' readiness to buy into Jesus when miracles were on offer, while nevertheless forsaking his teaching.

Nothing demonstrates their fickleness more than the events of Christ's passion. The week prior to the crucifixion began well enough with Jesus' celebrated entrance into Jerusalem. The crowds went before Jesus and followed him singing from Psalm 118, "Hosanna to the Son of David! Blessed is he who comes in the name of the Lord! Hosanna in the highest!" (Matthew 21:9). Perhaps at no point had they been greater, for they were an amalgam of two crowds—one, remarks William Hendrickson, which had followed Jesus from nearby Bethany, and the other from Jerusalem made up not only of inhabitants of the city but of those from Galilee who had made it to the city for the Feast of Passover. They had likely come out from Jerusalem to greet Jesus only to turn around to lead him into the city, singing as they went.[4]

Note, the significant spiritual irony going on here. The crowd cries out, "Hosanna to the Son of David!" thereby uncovering their mere lip service to Jesus. On the one hand, they acknowledged his royalty, referring to him as the promised descendant of David (cf., 2

---

[4] William Hendrickson, *The Gospel of Matthew*, reprint ed. (Edinburgh: The Banner of Truth Trust, 1976), 766.

Samuel 7:12). On the other hand, they cried out to him, "Hosanna . . .!" meaning "save now" or "save, pray." We would think, then, that they were praising God for their salvation, for what else is required of us than to call upon God that his Son, King Jesus, might save us. But not so fast! Their Hosanna chant reveals the startling reality that we can know the way of salvation and even pray for it or sing about it, and yet remain unsaved. Our trust, we recall, is not in the correctness of our understanding of salvation, in our prayers, or in our sung praise, yet none can expect to be saved who understand neither what they pray or sing, nor desire what God wants for them.

The events of Jesus' entrance into Jerusalem graphically portray, then, the pitfalls of cultural "Christianity" or churchianity. We may be present in public worship to recite the Apostles' Creed, we may know the way of salvation, we may even pray for it and sing about it, but without a changed heart we will remain unsaved. We are saved not because we have prayed a prayer, but because Christ in his majestic glory deigns to receive us. Think for a moment of the question we often ask people. It is a great question: "If you were to die today and God were to say to you, 'Why should I let you into my heaven?' What would you say?" To answer the question incorrectly is a sure sign that we have not understood the gospel. But it does not follow that we are authentically saved simply because we get the answer right (along the lines of, "Because Jesus has died for sinners" or even "Because Jesus has died for my sin").

The passion week proves this. As Jesus enters the city, Matthew tells us that "the whole city was stirred up, saying, 'Who is this?'" The crowds responded, "'This is the prophet Jesus, from Nazareth of Galilee,'" indicating that they knew something of Jesus' importance, and were not hostile to him as were the religious hierarchy. That said, by the end of the week they were siding with the religious authorities that Jesus should be crucified.

Although it took the betrayal of Judas to afford the religious hierarchy a way to get to Jesus (Matthew 26:14-15, 47-57), by the time his multilayered trial before the Sanhedrin, Herod, and Pilate was done, the crowds in Jerusalem were baying for his blood (Matthew 27:15-23). By offering them at the Feast of Passover a choice of the release of Jesus or Barabbas, Pilate likely hoped and anticipated that Jesus would be released. After all, Pilate had likely heard or recalled news of the "Hosanna" cries from five days earlier, had since found no guilt in Jesus (cf., John 19:4), and knew that it was for envy that he had been arrested (Matthew 27:18). Besides this, all knew that Barabbas was "a notorious prisoner" (Matthew 27:16).

How, then, do we account for the fickleness of the crowds? Matthew tells us: "The chief priests and the elders persuaded the crowd to ask for Barabbas and destroy Jesus" (v. 20). We do not know the arguments they employed. Perhaps they pulled rank as the religious authorities in the land, they claimed the longevity of their presence among the people, or, they pointed out that they were majority compared to Jesus' lone voice. Perhaps they made use of the false witnesses they had produced to condemn Jesus or argued pragmatically that whereas Jesus had failed to free them from the Romans, someone like Barabbas could pull that off. Whatever the line or lines of argument they used, it was all a sham. Pilate knew it, Jesus knew it, and so did the chief priests and elders.

Why then did the crowds buy into the hostility of the religious authorities, crying out repeatedly to Pilate, "Let him be crucified!"? It is quite simple. Their hearts were unchanged. So long as they remained so, they were liable to the winds of change. So are ours! People turn against Christ today once they deduce that they can no longer squeeze out of him what is in their self-interest, at least not without succumbing to his claim over their lives. Or, they reckon it is no longer in their best interests to be so closely allied to Jesus. Such an alliance is fine when Jesus is popular, but it proves to be a liability once the religious and the world join forces against him. After all, everyone wants to be on the winning side. The crowds failed to realize, however, that Christ's cross, resurrection, and ascension guarantee his victory for time and for eternity. Simply put, contrary to what they thought, they ended up on the wrong side of history.

The same goes for the crowds today. We are witnessing their fickleness with each passing day. After hundreds of years of enjoying the perks of Judeo-Christian values in society, brought about by the work of God in Christ through the spread of the gospel, the Reformation, and the successive revivals of the church, the crowds are being persuaded by small cliques of power to buy into anti-God and anti-Christ sentiments, whether the theory of evolution, abortion on demand, same-sex marriage, or transgenderism and the like. In no time, the followers of Christ are being marginalized, are losing their freedom of speech, and in some cases are threatened with the loss of their livelihoods. The crowds who once milled around Jesus in public worship, are quickly turning coat to side with today's haters of Jesus. Deducing prematurely that the capital of Christianity has run dry, they are throwing in their lot with those determined to destroy Jesus by destroying his church. Yet, they, too, shall end up on the losing side of history. On the last day, there Jesus will stand, the sole victor on the battlefield of time, surrounded by a myriad of admiring and devoted followers who, across the centuries and the world, have surrendered their lives to him and have felt the benefits of doing so (2 Thessalonians 1:10). Those benefits are innumerable, but the one most fitting to mention is the freedom Christ's rule affords us from having to comply with every fad or "ism" which passes our way.

HOW WE ANSWER

So, we come back to the question as to whether we are in the crowd or in the kingdom; whether ours is a cultural "Christianity" amounting to but a mere outward churchianity, or an authentic biblical and spiritual Christianity. In the question lies, then, the timely challenge posed by Jesus' parable.

Our response to Jesus must be all the more a matter of faith than was the case with the apostles and the disciples, since we have no personal experience of him in the flesh nor of his earthly ministry. Yet, Peter, thinking back on the transfiguration of Christ and the voice he heard from heaven (cf., Matthew 17:5), underlined the value of Scripture, telling his readers that we have "something more sure, the prophetic word, to which [we] do well to pay attention as to a lamp shining in a dark place, until the day dawns and the morning star rises in [our] hearts" (2 Peter 1:19).

In Scripture we get to read of how the kingdom came, of its establishment by the death, resurrection, and ascension of Jesus, and of Christ's sending forth of the Holy Spirit. Christianese may not doubt all this for a moment and yet, at best, trusts solely in the trustworthiness of Scripture. This trust affords but a notional knowledge of Christ. For the authentic Christian, confidence in the trustworthiness of the Scriptures is just the beginning of saving faith, for knowledge or *notitia* is but its first element. If that is all we have, then ours is but an intellectual faith (a skeletal trust in the facts of the gospel). Saving faith includes not only knowledge of the gospel, but conviction concerning our personal need of it (*assensus*) and a wholehearted trust (*fiducia*) in the Christ of Scripture for personal salvation. Hence Keach's distinction between a notional and an experiential knowledge. Only authentic Christians, possessing saving faith (all three elements of knowledge [*notitia*], conviction [*assensus*], and trust [*fiducia*]), can claim for themselves Jesus' wonderful blessing of his disciples: ". . . blessed are your eyes for they see, and your ears for they hear" (Matthew 13:16). It means all the more to us, given our Lord's sympathy for those he knew would believe on him without seeing him in person. "Blessed," he said to

Thomas, "are those who have not seen [me] and yet have believed" (John 20:29).

If you have yet to come to Christ and to enter his kingdom but would like this blessing—the blessing of a Savior for your forgiveness, and a King for your guidance into ways pleasing to God—know that Jesus, as Savior, warmly invites you to come to him, and, as King, lovingly commands you to do so. He promises that none who do are rejected.

I leave you, then, with three pieces of counsel. These I offer you tenderly.

First, hear the Word.

To hear the Word is to put yourself under the Word. You say, "I already attend church." Well, consistent with what we have heard from Jesus' parable, it is important not only to hear the words stated there, but to begin to listen to them. If you are privileged enough to go to a church where the Word of God is faithfully taught, then let the weight of the Word preached rest on your mind and begin to seep down into your heart. Is the minister inviting you to come in faith to Christ, then come! Is he through the Word commanding you to come, then come! Let the Word float over your head no more, nor let it drift in one ear and out of the other. If there are aspects of the sermons or Bible studies you do not understand, then ask. Ask as you would a matter that is one of life or death, and don't stop asking unless or until you find answers that accord with God's Word and satisfy your soul.

If, however, you have picked up this book "by chance," but have no habit of attending church, I encourage you to find a forum in which you, too, can hear God's Word, and on its own terms. Write to us at From His Fullness for your free quarterly copy of *The Way* (fromhisfullness@mail.com), to Reaching America Ministries for relevant literature (try the *Freedom from* series [www.reachingamerica.net/neighborhood-outreach-resources]). To go further, look out for introductory courses on Christianity (notably *Christianity Explored* [www.christianityexplored.com]), or a Bible study group where you can make friends and learn more of the gospel in community with those willing to field your questions. Ultimately, though, you will want to begin your search for a church family wherein God's Word is treasured, heard, and followed. God uses his people to introduce others to the hearing of the Word. Translators translate it, theologians teach it, preachers preach it, and family and friends help us find our way around it. And once under the Word, follow the invitation given to come to Christ. No one who does, ever regrets it.

Be assured that faithful churches are looking to get the Word of God to you. Do not fear, then, connecting with a local church. Stick with your new friends who emphasize Scripture and the gospel and are equipped and willing to meet you where you are at. If, however, you are unable to find a church or help, do not despair. Many have come to faith and repentance reading the Scriptures on their own. This should not surprise us. God is sovereign and rules and overrules in the circumstances of life in order to bring us to himself. Since he calls us to hear his Word, he is well able to help us find a way to do that. But there is also an onus on you to go looking for the Word and, having found it, to read and to listen to what God has to say to you through it. The opportunities to do so today are just about limitless: hard copy, online versions, kindle, apps, audio Bibles, study Bibles, and braille Bibles, etc.

Know that this is essential.[5] In the Holy Scriptures God reveals to us how our lives have either degenerated into gross sin and its inevitable dysfunction and enslavement, or how our attempt

---

[5] The WCF, a faithful summary of biblical teaching, allows for only two cases in which God may call apart from the use of his Word: that of the unborn and the mentally impaired (10:3).

to live an orderly life has bred a legalistic lifelessness which, failing to achieve perfection before God and to satisfy his justice, can never procure our entrance into Christ's kingdom. Said Jesus, "unless your righteousness exceeds that of the scribes and Pharisees, you will never enter the kingdom" (Matthew 5:20; cf., 18:3). Rather, entrance into the kingdom is richly provided for all those who, facing up to the bad news about themselves, come, by God's grace, to appreciate the wonderful news of the kingdom (2 Peter 1:11).

Whether we come at the Scriptures as irreligious and/or dysfunctional, or religious but legalistic, they duly humble us before God. None of us welcomes this. Indeed, Satan preys on the pain of our humbling to tempt us to forsake our seeking of the kingdom. Remember, though, that Jesus said we must become like children if we are to enter it (Matthew 18:2-4). Children understand that they know little and are full of questions. But it is as we position ourselves as children before God that he shares with us the most wonderful news there is, namely, that he loves us and stands ready to forgive our sins no matter their gravity, and to refashion our lives into something beautiful and useful for the spread of the kingdom of heaven.

Second, embrace Christ.

The blessings God offers us are not automatic. They come only to those embracing Christ as their Savior and King. Recall that Jesus told his parable of the sower on his way to the cross.

The cross was both Christ's destiny and the cause of much misunderstanding in Israel. The King for whom God's ancient people looked turned out to be different from the liberator from Roman oppression many of them craved. It was easy enough for them to attribute historical prophecies of the glory of the coming King to the Messiah, but the glory they had in mind differed from what God was envisioning when he sent the prophets to foretell of the Messiah. Whereas God foresaw the Messiah entering his glory

214

through his prior sufferings, the people of Israel assumed that prophetic references of suffering pertained to their circumstances since they had suffered so much over the centuries.

Thus, when Jesus died, the spirits of the apostles and disciples plummeted into despair and disbelief. Notwithstanding his forewarnings that his sufferings would precede his glorification (Matthew 16:21-23; 17:22-23; 20:17-19), they failed to realize that his agonizing death was itself a glorification of God's mercy and grace in atoning for sinners and was the prelude to the wonder of his resurrection. Raised the third day following his death, Jesus set about lifting the spirits of his disciples and correcting their understanding of the Scriptures.

Think of Jesus' appearance to Cleopas and his fellow traveler (whether his wife or another disciple). Feeling defeated and let down, they forsook Jerusalem and made their way down the road to Emmaus. Joining them unannounced as they made their way along the route of sixty stadia (seven miles), Jesus led them through a prolonged Bible study (Luke 24:25-31), later repeating the same to the remainder of the disciples hanging around in Jerusalem (Luke 24:44-49). The sufferings of which the Old Testament prophecies spoke were indeed those of the Messiah. By shedding his blood unto the death of the cross, Jesus, it turned out, had broken the power of Satan and, freeing his people from the kingdom of darkness, had opened the way for them to enter his heavenly kingdom, leaving behind their domain of darkness (Colossians 1:13).

You, too, may know this deliverance and transference. The blood Christ shed as Savior from the cross is the means of your forgiveness, and his reign over your heart as resurrected King is the means of your freedom from sin—not only its guilt (immediately), but also its power (gradually), and its presence (eternally). Such blessings are given to any and to all who, reading of Christ in his Word, embrace him wholly as their personal Savior and King. We cannot own him as one but not the other, for the two offices are inseparably connected in Christ.

The spotlight, however, is not all on Christ. There is a divine spotlight on us, too, scanning our sincerity in processing Christ's call to enter his kingdom.

If we say we are ready to embrace Christ as Savior but not as King, it is certain we are not ready at all. For it is disingenuous to want his forgiveness but not the freedom he offers us from the sins for which we say we are contrite. Once we know what our sins mean to God and what they cost Christ, forgiveness cannot come soon enough; and once we have our eyes opened to how much purposelessness, emptiness, havoc, and ruin sin has brought to our lives we yearn for their refashioning by the power and authority of Christ before any more of our days ebb away.

Alternatively, if we say we are willing to embrace Christ as both Savior and King but prefer to leave off doing so until the end of our lives, we need to get real with ourselves. Such talk is both foolish and selfish. It is foolish, because we don't know how our last days will play out. They may end in the blink of an eye, or in protracted months and years of unconsciousness or senility. It is selfish, because we were created to live not for ourselves but for God's higher purposes. Selfishness is, then, self-defeating. Paradoxically, it is in fulfilling God's purposes for our lives that we find our greatest contentment and enjoyment in life.

If you are already at life's end—your years or state of health guaranteeing this—don't despair nor let the devil, who is the enemy of your soul, tell you otherwise. There is a reason, likely plenty of them, why the account of the thief on the cross is included in Scripture. As he hung there dying, unable to undo his past, to make up for it, or to undertake a single work to atone for his sin (not that he could have, had he his whole life before him), he could do nothing else but look to Jesus. The simplicity of his faith has such beauty: "Jesus, remember me when you come into your kingdom." Not impressed by the long, grandstanding, self-righteous prayers of the Pharisees (cf., Luke 18:11-14), Jesus answered him, "Truly, I say to you, today you shall be with me in Paradise" (Luke 23:42). Jesus referred to the unseen realm his subjects enter upon death, namely, heaven.[6]

Therefore, in love, in Christ's name, and with much prayer, I appeal to you to embrace him. The kingdom provided for you, is nevertheless that into which God calls you (1 Thessalonians 2:12). Don't, then, trample the seed of God's Word under foot, or allow the devil and his demons to snatch it from your heart, or permit the thorns of your heart to preclude the seed from growing. Instead, embrace Christ! He promises to protect and to nurture the imperishable seed sown in your heart, to drive from you the evil one, and to replace your stony heart with a new one. Don't delay. "Harvest time," to quote Billy Graham, "is the ever-present now"! Christ stands ready, willing, and able to hear your prayer. The border post at the entrance of the kingdom is open to you who turn to God through Christ. You are invited to bow before him now while you may, before the awesome royal majesty of Christ scheduled for cosmic display at the end of the age determines you must (cf., Philippians 2:10-11).

Third, rejoice in Christ's reign.

Relinquishing our cherished rule over our own lives is the last thing we would do, left to ourselves. Yet, in conversion we relinquish it definitively, and progressively thereafter the more we mature in Christ. Under the tutelage of God's Word and Spirit we

---

[6] The heaven that currently exists in its intermediate state portends heaven in its final state which shall be inaugurated when Christ returns. His return will indicate the fulfillment of his mediatorial kingdom and shall occasion his royal judgment of all, whether living or dead (2 Timothy 4:1).

discern one area of our lives after another in which God has not been glorified because Christ has been shut out of reigning therein. By his tutelage God graciously and lovingly calls us to surrender increasingly our rights and to open our hearts to him more and more. It is in this way that Christ extends his rule over our hearts and takes ever increasing ownership of the details of our lives. To the person who loves sin this is unthinkable, but to the one who has come to see sin and folly for what it is, there is genuine delight in their growing acquaintance with Christ and his ways. To know Christ is to want more of him. To enter his kingdom is to realize that in its countercultural values is found the very meaning and purpose God designed for our lives.

Two main factors encourage us to surrender our lives to Christ.

First, there is the jadedness we feel on account of our sins. Whereas once they symbolized our rights and liberties, the harsh school of experience has taught us under the good hand of God, that our sins have been, to one degree and another, but an anarchic, self-defeating rebellion. The trophies handed out by sin include emptiness and guilt. These are often accompanied by ruin and wreckage, whether spiritual, emotional, or physical, or the total trifecta. Against such a backdrop of consequent misery, dysfunction, self-loathing, and insecurity the promise of true freedom and hope in Christ becomes attractive to us. Our surrender to Christ is, then, retrospectively and inwardly influenced.

Second, our surrender is also prospectively and outwardly encouraged. Not only does Christ's royal power subdue our hearts, guarding us from their betrayal and the self-harm they inflict, his royal protection shields us from the world of sin and enmity against God, and from his archenemy the Devil who is so bent on our destruction. The more, then, that we learn of Christ and of the benefits of surrendering to him, the more we delight in Christ and detect the joy our surrender brings to him and to ourselves. It is under his reign that life, liberty, and the pursuit of happiness become a reality. The life Christ offers is eternal, the liberty he has purchased for us is safe, and the pursuit of happiness he facilitates ensures us an unending satisfaction in God. Thus, with Thor Harris we sing:

> Who can cheer the heart like Jesus,
> By His presence all divine?
> True and tender, pure and precious,
> O how blest to call Him mine!
> All that thrills my soul is Jesus;
> He is more than life to me;
> And the fairest of ten thousand
> In my blessed Lord I see.

What is more, in Christ we get to enlist in a cause so much greater than ourselves. The delight we experience through the spread of Christ's reign within is a profound catalyst for the longing of members of the kingdom to see the reign of Christ spread throughout the world. The further the kingdom of heaven extends, with one person after another coming to repentance and faith, the more we rejoice. It does our hearts good to know that others are also getting to see how majestic Christ is. After all, it is fitting that he who is a great Christ should have a great following, and it is thrilling to learn how one people group after another is being reached, so heralding thereby the promised return of the King (Matthew 24:14). All citizens of the kingdom can thus sing, no matter their eschatology (understanding of the last things):

> Jesus shall reign where'er the sun
> Does his successive journeys run;
> His kingdom stretch from shore to shore,
> Till moons shall wax and wane no more,
> Till moons shall wax and wane no more.[7]

---

[7] Isaac Watts' 1719 paraphrase of Psalm 72.

Yes, God's people can be negligent in preaching the Word of the kingdom and deficient in portraying it, Satan opposes Christ's kingdom, the Pharisees and scribes set up roadblocks to hinder entrance into it (Matthew 23:13), and men and women reject it. But the kingdom, for all its setbacks in various places and times, continues to grow and to spread. We rejoice even now, and notwithstanding our Lord's parable of the sower, that the kingdom of the world is becoming the kingdom of our Lord and of his Christ, and he shall reign forever and ever (Revelation 11:15).

"He," then, "who has ears, let him hear" (Matthew 13:9). In Jesus' directive to listen to him there is no pun at work—the Greek words for *ears* of the body and ears of corn differ. Nevertheless, who can deny that if we have ears to hear Jesus we will, no matter who we are, bring forth ears of corn. We close, then, with prayer to this end, quoting the hymn of John Cawood (1819):

> Almighty God, your word is cast
> Like seed into the ground;
> Now let the dew of heav'n descend,
> And righteous fruits abound.
>
> Let not the foe of Christ and man
> This holy seed remove,
> But give it root in every heart
> To bring forth fruits of love.
>
> Let not the world's deceitful cares
> The rising plant destroy,
> But let it yield a hundredfold
> The fruits of peace and joy.
>
> Oft as the precious seed is sown,
> Your quickening grace bestow,
> That all whose souls the truth receive,
> Its saving power may know.

STUDY QUESTIONS: SESSION EIGHT

1. How does the sowing of the seed of God's Word in the apostolic era both encourage and challenge you regarding the sowing we are called of God to undertake today?

2. Have you known an officebearer in the church to betray the Lord? While not gossiping the details, discuss how the subsequent history of the Lord and his apostles encourages you to move toward your recovery/the recovery of your Christian community.

3. As Christianity decreases in popularity in the West, we see false disciples forsaking the church. Discuss how we distinguish someone backsliding and needing recovery from those who were never converted. When do we chase after them and when do we let them go?

4. Despite the parables' indication of the impending judgment on the crowds, Jesus continued to look in compassion on them and to serve their needs. Discuss the dynamics involved in helping those who refuse to enter the kingdom or who procrastinate in doing so.

5. What is your assurance that you are a citizen of Christ's kingdom rather than just a member of the crowd? What biblical criteria factor into your assurance? If you were arrested for being a Christian, what external evidence would be used against you?

6. If you are yet to enter the kingdom of heaven, can you identify what holds you back? Is there help you need from the Christian community/help we can offer seekers as citizens of the kingdom?

Prayer: Lord God, we thank you for Jesus' parable of the sower. Having heard it, glorify your name by our listening to it and by the fruit to come from our having done so. In the name of King Jesus, we pray. Amen.

SELECT READING

Here are a few of the sources cited to read further about the kingdom of heaven, the parables, and living all out for Christ:

Introductory:

Bilkes, Gerald M. *Glory Veiled and Unveiled: A Heart-Searching Look at Christ's Parables* (Grand Rapids: Reformation Heritage Books, 2012).

Lloyd-Jones, D. Martyn. *The Kingdom of God* (Cambridge: Crossway Books, 1992).

Platt, David. *Radical: Taking Back Your Faith from the American Dream* (Colorado Springs, Colorado: Multnomah Books, 2011).

Lengthier:

Hanko, Herman C. *The Mysteries of the Kingdom: An Exposition of the Parables* (Grand Rapids: Reformed Free Publishing Association, 1975).

Keach, Benjamin. *Exposition of the Parables*, Series One, reprint ed. (Grand Rapids: Kregel Publications, 1991).

Ridderbos, Herman. *The Coming of the Kingdom.* Transl. H. de Jongste, ed. Raymond O. Zorn (Phillipsburg, NJ: P&R, 1962).

From His Fullness *envisions God's pleasure in the feeding of the hungriest church leaders and their congregations across the world with the grace and truth of the Living Word, through the written Word.*

Specifically, From His Fullness Ministries exists to:

- Offer affordable theological educational to pastors *in situ* in areas of the world where there is significant growth for the church but minimal resources. This offer includes ministry to women by Brenda Trumper, a member of the board of directors and manager of From His Fullness Ministries.

- Encourage community outreach among pastors and their congregations especially in areas of the world where secularism is eroding the Judeo-Christian values of society and where the foundations need rebuilding.

For further information or to donate to this worthy cause, go to www.fromhisfullness.com or write to fromhisfullness@mail.com. You may also follow the ministry through the From His Fullness Facebook page.

The Way

JUNE 2018 EDITION

Good News for a Groaning World   *Issue No. 1*

FIFA WORLD CUP
RUSSIA 2018

The Beautiful Game!

Occurring every four years, this World Cup (June 14 through July 15) is the twenty-first and, once more, will be the most viewed sporting event in the world. Consider that in 2014, when the event was held in Brazil, 3.2 billion people out of a world population of over 7 billion tuned in to the tournament. From here in America where the millions of American fans in an era when two of the greatest players in the history of the game are fighting it out to be the undisputed greatest. Both of them need to lead their team to victory to settle the matter, but only one of them can. The stage is set!

Who Will Lose?

This is all good fun, for Christians, too. But, to many, football is so much more than that. It is a religion and an idol (a substitute for God). The players are the high priests, the game is the savior, the supporters are the devotees, the chants are the hymns, and

ON OFFER TO YOU!

Free to you each quarter for your community—From His Fullness Ministries' outreach publication *The Way*! Write to fromhisfullness@mail.com stating your preferences:

- General copy for direct distribution and/or the master copy for customized distribution by your church or ministry.

- English (*The Way*), Spanish (*El Camino*), or Italian (*Il Cammino*).

Go to www.fromhisfullness.com for options for distribution: by hard copy mailing, email distribution, or upload to your website.

El CAMINO

EDICION MARZO 2019

Personalize su frase en este espacio   *Ejemplar No. 4*

LAS FALSAS NOTICIAS NO SE PUEDEN FINGIR

Aquí está la ironía: las noticias falsas son reales. ¡Muy real! Oh, la frase puede ser nueva, popularizada durante la elección presidencial de los EE. UU. De 2016 por Donald Trump, pero la difusión de noticias falsas, ya sea por sátira , por desinformación intencional o similar, es tan antigua como las colinas. Literalmente, se remonta a los albores de la historia, cuando Satanás engañó a Eva con un relato falso de lo que

Goebbels del cine para propaganda. "El Maestro de las Mentiras" afirmó que una mentira repetida mil veces se convierte en la verdad. Sin embargo, las dictaduras no están solas en falsificar información. Los medios estatales están separados solo por grados de las noticias políticamente partidistas de hoy.

El advenimiento de las redes sociales ha hecho que la difusión de la información errónea, la información errónea y la

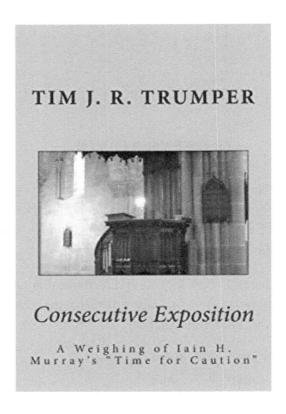

Made in the USA
Monee, IL
10 December 2020

51966540R00152